Mobile JavaScript Application Development

Adrian Kosmaczewski

Beijing · Cambridge · Farnham · Köln · Sebastopol · Tokyo

Mobile JavaScript Application Development
by Adrian Kosmaczewski

Published by O'Reilly Media, Inc., 1005 Gravenstein Highway North, Sebastopol, CA 95472.

O'Reilly books may be purchased for educational, business, or sales promotional use. Online editions are also available for most titles (*http://my.safaribooksonline.com*). For more information, contact our corporate/institutional sales department: 800-998-9938 or *corporate@oreilly.com*.

Editor: Simon St. Laurent	**Cover Designer:** Karen Montgomery
Production Editor: Melanie Yarbrough	**Interior Designer:** David Futato
	Illustrator: Robert Romano

Revision History for the First Edition:
    2012-06-14   First release
See *http://oreilly.com/catalog/errata.csp?isbn=9781449327859* for release details.

ISBN: 978-1-449-32785-9

[LSI]

1339700763

Table of Contents

Preface

Introduction

The most important current trend in the software development world is, without a hint of a doubt, the *mobile frontier*, and in particular, the rise of the smartphone and the touch tablet.

When I started my career as a developer, back in 1996, I was writing web applications running on Netscape Navigator 3 and Internet Explorer 3[1]. The world was a very different place back then, particularly in this industry. I used HoTMetaL Pro and Notepad to code my pages, as well as the editor bundled with Netscape Navigator.

Since then I have written applications for both the web and the desktop, using technologies such as Classic ASP, VBScript, ASP.NET, PHP, C+\+, Ruby on Rails, Django, etc. For my editing needs, I have migrated to EditPlus, later TextMate, now Vim[2].

But without any doubt, the most important moment in recent technological history was the introduction of the iPhone in January 2007. The impressive growths of iOS, Android, and other platforms has completely transformed the landscape of software engineering, while at the same time opening new possibilities for companies. The rise of the iPhone was followed by the explosion of the Android platform, and in all that turmoil, BlackBerry and Windows Mobile have lost their leadership, even if they still remain relevant in the current landscape.

This new panorama has a darker side, one already known in the desktop development world: *platform fragmentation*.

Fragmentation

The latest statistics at the time of this writing indicate that Android is leading the smartphone race with more than 51% of all sales in the last quarter of 2011, with iOS holding around 43% during the same period. BlackBerry, once the biggest name in the

---

1. I'm not really fond of those times, mind you.
2. Some of you might think that I have travelled back in time. Well, in a sense, you are right!

smartphone world, accounted for less than 6%, while Windows Phone, Bada, and Symbian, together with other more or less known platforms, shared the remaining percentage points[3].

These numbers clearly show that the smartphone market is very different from the PC market; there is not really a winner (at least not at the time of this writing), and companies wanting to take advantage of this new communication channel have to make substantial investments in order to be present in as many pockets as possible. Many applications have to be written in at least two or three platforms (usually iOS, Android, and BlackBerry) to reach a sizeable chunk of the market.

In any case, the smartphone is poised to take over the cellphone market in years to come; at the end of 2010, 10% of the mobile phone market was dominated by smartphones, with a yearly growth of more than 100%. The most pessimistic statistics indicate that by 2013 more than 50% of the mobile phone market will be dominated by smartphones, most of them featuring a touchscreen. This figure has been reached in the USA, where more than 50% of all mobile phones can be considered "smartphones" since February 2012[4].

A lot has changed since 2007, indeed. But, just like in the case of its desktop counterpart, the Web appears like the most important cross-platform solution available to software engineers today.

Growth of the Mobile Web

One of the breakthroughs of this new breed of mobile devices is the availability of fully fledged mobile web browsers , supporting most of the current standards like HTML5, CSS, JavaScript, and many other standard technologies. Many of us remember watching Steve Jobs demonstrating the capabilities of the Mobile Safari browser in the first iPhone, recognizing that a new era had started precisely that day. Mobile browsers should not only be as capable as their desktop counterparts, they had features beyond the imaginable, they were fast, and they were fully standards-compliant.

The growth in power of the mobile web has brought new possibilities; particularly in countries with low penetration of technology, like Latin America or Africa, smartphones appear like a cheaper way[5] to access online information and services. For example, in 2010, more than 30% of all web access from Africa was made through a smartphone[6]; in Latin America, this number fluctuates between 10% and 15%. All of these countries have seen a huge increase in the proportion of web content consumed

---

3. Source: TechCrunch (*http://techcrunch.com/2012/01/09/ios-marketshare-up-from-26-in-q3-to-43-in -octnov-2011/*).

4. Source: Nielsen Wire (*http://blog.nielsen.com/nielsenwire/online_mobile/smartphones-account-for-half-of -all-mobile-phones-dominate-new-phone-purchases-in-the-us/*)

5. At least, cheaper than buying a laptop!

through smartphones in the latest years, following the progression in power and capabilities of these new devices.

Worldwide, the average web usage proportion on mobile devices was around 8% at the time of this writing[7], a huge increase from the 1.5% in 2009. It is estimated that, in 2015, more than 50% of all web requests will come from mobile devices!

New Paradigms

All of this represents a huge shift in our software development habits, a radical change from the usual wisdom that states that the mobile web is just an afterthought; today, we have to see the mobile site as the primary channel of our web presence, because the usage of the web from the desktop is going to be eventually lower than that of the mobile web.

But this new perspective raises a few questions, too:

- How many platforms do I have to test my sites in?
- Do I have to care about low-end mobile phones?
- Which libraries can I use to speed up my developments?
- What is the level of standard support in the major mobile browsers?

This book will provide some answers to these questions. In particular, it will take an opinionated, hands-on approach to help you quickly solve problems and find answers as fast as possible.

To do that, we are going to concentrate our efforts in the following technologies, which are currently the most promising and which show the most interesting roadmap:

- PhoneGap
- Sencha Touch
- jQuery Mobile

Even if this book is centered around these technologies, this does not mean that there are not other, very promising and interesting technologies available for you to try; here are some names and links that might interest you: SproutCore (*http://www.sproutcore .com/*), iWebKit (*http://snippetspace.com/*), WebApp.net (*http://webapp-net.com/*), jQTouch (*http://jqtouch.com/*), Jo (*http://joapp.com/*), iUI (*http://code.google.com/p/ iui/*), and zepto.js (*http://zeptojs.com/*). We are not, however, going to talk about them in this book.

---

6. Source: "The Great Rise of the Mobile Web" at The Next Web. (*http://thenextweb.com/mobile/2011/01/ 06/the-great-rise-of-the-mobile-web/:*)

7. Source: StatCounter Global Stats (*http://gs.statcounter.com/#mobile_vs_desktop-ww-monthly-201111 -201204-bar*)

At the end of this book, Bibliography contains a long list of references, including books and websites, that you can use as reference for your future developments.

We are also going to pay attention to many other aspects of application development, including testing and debugging, providing a quick overview of the most relevant techniques and tools available for mobile web developers today.

Who Should Read This Book

This book is tailored for web developers familiar with the following technologies:

- HTML
- CSS
- JavaScript

It does not matter if you have mobile software engineering experience, but of course if you do, well, it will be a huge help! Mobile applications are a world of their own, and they present challenges that common desktop applications don't deal with, such as:

- Small screen sizes
- Reduced battery life
- Little memory and disk specifications
- Rapidly changing networking conditions

This book deals only with client-side considerations (apart from some exceptions regarding HTML5 application manifests) so developers should be able to apply the techniques and frameworks shown in this book with any server-side technology.

Book Structure

When going through the pages of this book, you are going to see that the core motivation behind these pages is to help you *understand by doing*. We are going to leave the theory to others, and we are going to concentrate our efforts into writing code and trying to become better at creating web applications.

This Book Is About "Web Apps"

Please pay attention to the fact that this book focuses on the creation of *web applications for touch screen smartphones*, not simple websites; although web applications use the same tools and languages as normal websites, there are important differences in terms of usability, monetization, marketing, and distribution that must be taken into account. Web applications also have important consequences in the enterprise world, which we are going to discuss as well in this book.

The first chapter, Chapter 1 begins by providing an introduction to HTML5 from the perspective of the mobile application developer. The chapter goes through the major features introduced by the latest version of the HTML standard, including the application cache, the new tags, and the new APIs exposed by modern mobile browsers.

Then, Chapter 2 provides an overview of advanced concepts such as object orientation, closures and the importance of coding conventions. The idea is to highlight common "gotchas" that dazzle developers coming from other languages such as Java or C#.

Then we are going to dive into the real subject, and we are going to use Sencha Touch and jQuery Mobile to write the same kind of application (namely, a "to do list" kind of app) using both. This will help you understand how different these two technologies are, and how you have to adapt your mindset to each in order to achieve your goals.

Chapter 3 will introduce you to one of the hottest mobile application frameworks of the moment; this chapter will provide an introduction to the core concepts, the available widgets, and will guide the reader in the development of a creation of a "to do list" kind of application.

Chapter 4 will take you to the core concepts behind one of the most powerful JavaScript frameworks available today. We are going to review the architecture, widgets and idioms required to build Sencha Touch applications.

Finally, we are going to wrap these applications in the Chapter 5 chapter, to be deployed as a native iOS, Android or Windows Phone application; we are going to learn how to do that, and which other capabilities PhoneGap brings to the table as well.

The book ends with a chapter called Chapter 6, providing tips and tricks to enable developers to increase the quality of their applications, using the latest and best tools available.

What You Need

The code samples in this book were created using OS X 10.7 "Lion", and were tested on iOS and Android devices running the latest software versions available at the time of this writing (iOS 5, Android 4).

As for software, the sample applications were written on Mac OS X "Lion" using Vim (*http://www.vim.org*), MacVim (*http://code.google.com/p/macvim/*) with the Janus (*https://github.com/carlhuda/janus*) extensions and some other modifications by the author of this book (*http://github.com/akosmasoftware/dotfiles*), and were then converted into native applications using PhoneGap. They were deployed using the following IDEs:

- Xcode 4.3
- IntelliJ IDEA Community Edition
- Eclipse
- Visual Studio Express for Windows Phone

We will be using both Eclipse and IDEA to show how to create native Android apps with web technologies, and Visual Studio Express will help us create them for Windows Phone 7.

It is also recommended to use a local development web server; for example the one bundled with your operating system, or for greater flexibility on OS X, we recommend using MAMP (*http://www.mamp.info/en/index.html*).

The usual web developer workflow consists of an endless series of edit-save-refresh sequences; to simplify our work, I recommend using a tool like LiveReload (*http://livereload.com/*) (available in the Mac App Store) which provides a simple mechanism, and reloads automatically any browser connected to a particular web app.

Finally, a fundamental element are simulators and emulators. The Android emulator (shown in Figure P-2) is bundled with the standard Android SDK (*http://developer.android.com/sdk/index.html*), available from Google. As for the iOS Simulator (shown in Figure P-1), it is available with the free iOS SDK (*http://developer.apple.com/ios*) and the developer tools available from Apple (which are also available when downloading Xcode for free from the Mac App Store).

To access the local web server from these emulators and simulators, use the following URLs:

- From the iOS Simulator (shown in Figure P-1), you can use "http://localhost" (and the corresponding port, for example "8888" for MAMP)
- From the Android Emulator (shown in Figure P-2), use the IP "10.0.2.2"

Figure P-1. iOS Simulator

Code of the Book

You can download all the code samples of this book from Github (*https://github.com/ akosma/Mobile-JavaScript-Application-Development*). The project contains an installation script named install.sh that will download all the required libraries for the samples to run; it will also get a copy of the PhoneGap Kitchen Sink Project (*https:// github.com/jcfischer/pgkitchensink*) by Jens-Christian Fischer, which is described in detail in Chapter 5.

Figure P-2. Android Emulator

The code of the book is distributed using a liberal BSD license, and will be updated in the future to reflect the changes and updates to the libraries used.

Acknowledgements

This book would not have been possible without the help of countless software developers, who spend days and nights in front of their computers to create the amazing pieces of software that make up our world. In particular, Github (*http://github.com*) and Stack Overflow (*http://stackoverflow.com*) are probably the most important sources of information for software developers ever created. My thanks to the amazing teams behind those systems. You rock.

Thanks to Mats Bryntse from bryntum.com (*http://www.bryntum.com/*), who provided a pre-release copy of his Siesta testing framework, including Sencha Touch 2 support.

I am also in debt to the many people who have read and commented on the early drafts of this book: first to my editor, Simon St. Laurent, who has provided guidance and feedback during the whole process. To Maximiliano Firtman, who has been instrumental in providing me with the contact with O'Reilly, and who has clearly brought order to the world of the mobile web. To Jens-Christian Fischer, with whom I have had the tremendous privilege of setting up an unprecedented series of successful mobile web trainings in Zürich. To Bertrand Dufresne, organizer of the JavaScript Genève developer group, and whose @jsgeneve Twitter account (*http://twitter.com/jsgeneve*) has been an endless stream of inspiration. To Anice Hassim and Kishyr Ramdial from immedia, South Africa, met a cold morning of April 2010 while waiting to buy our first iPads in NYC, and with whom we have organized countless training sessions around the mobile web in South Africa. And finally to Gabriel Garcia Marengo, who has read the manuscript and provided great feedback.

But most important, I want to thank my wife, Claudia, for without her there is no possible happiness.

Conventions Used in This Book

The following typographical conventions are used in this book:

Italic
> Indicates new terms, URLs, email addresses, filenames, and file extensions.

`Constant width`
> Used for program listings, as well as within paragraphs to refer to program elements such as variable or function names, databases, data types, environment variables, statements, and keywords.

`Constant width bold`
> Shows commands or other text that should be typed literally by the user.

`Constant width italic`
> Shows text that should be replaced with user-supplied values or by values determined by context.

 This icon signifies a tip, suggestion, or general note.

 This icon indicates a warning or caution.

Using Code Examples

This book is here to help you get your job done. In general, you may use the code in this book in your programs and documentation. You do not need to contact us for permission unless you're reproducing a significant portion of the code. For example, writing a program that uses several chunks of code from this book does not require permission. Selling or distributing a CD-ROM of examples from O'Reilly books does require permission. Answering a question by citing this book and quoting example code does not require permission. Incorporating a significant amount of example code from this book into your product's documentation does require permission.

We appreciate, but do not require, attribution. An attribution usually includes the title, author, publisher, and ISBN. For example: "*Mobile JavaScript Application Development* by Adrian Kosmaczewski (O'Reilly). Copyright 2012 Adrian Kosmaczewski, 978-1-449-32785-9."

If you feel your use of code examples falls outside fair use or the permission given above, feel free to contact us at *permissions@oreilly.com*.

Safari® Books Online

Safari Safari Books Online (*www.safaribooksonline.com*) is an on-demand digital library that delivers expert content in both book and video form from the world's leading authors in technology and business.

Technology professionals, software developers, web designers, and business and creative professionals use Safari Books Online as their primary resource for research, problem solving, learning, and certification training.

Safari Books Online offers a range of product mixes and pricing programs for organizations, government agencies, and individuals. Subscribers have access to thousands of books, training videos, and prepublication manuscripts in one fully searchable database from publishers like O'Reilly Media, Prentice Hall Professional, Addison-Wesley Professional, Microsoft Press, Sams, Que, Peachpit Press, Focal Press, Cisco Press, John Wiley & Sons, Syngress, Morgan Kaufmann, IBM Redbooks, Packt, Adobe Press, FT Press, Apress, Manning, New Riders, McGraw-Hill, Jones & Bartlett, Course Technology, and dozens more. For more information about Safari Books Online, please visit us online.

How to Contact Us

Please address comments and questions concerning this book to the publisher:

O'Reilly Media, Inc.
1005 Gravenstein Highway North
Sebastopol, CA 95472
800-998-9938 (in the United States or Canada)
707-829-0515 (international or local)
707-829-0104 (fax)

We have a web page for this book, where we list errata, examples, and any additional information. You can access this page at:

http://oreil.ly/mobile_JS_appdev

To comment or ask technical questions about this book, send email to:

bookquestions@oreilly.com

For more information about our books, courses, conferences, and news, see our website at *http://www.oreilly.com*.

Find us on Facebook: *http://facebook.com/oreilly*

Follow us on Twitter: *http://twitter.com/oreillymedia*

Watch us on YouTube: *http://www.youtube.com/oreillymedia*

CHAPTER 1

HTML5 for Mobile Applications

This chapter will introduce some basic concepts about HTML5, and will explain the impact of the new features of the standard in mobile applications. We are going to see how different aspects of HTML5 are brought together, how they impact our markup code, and how they can be used in a mobile environment.

A Bit of History

HTML5 was born as a reaction to the direction that the W3C was giving to the HTML 5 standards (note the difference in the names, one with a space, the other without). The HTML5 standard, proposed by the WHATWG group, primarily proposed by Opera, Mozilla, and Apple, was designed with the core principle of *simplification* of the whole HTML specification.

Another important element of the HTML5 specification is the strong focus in applications . Apple and others providers have foreseen, five years ago, the implications and opportunities provided by a standardized, distributed, simplified application development framework, available in every mobile device on the planet, and they have pushed forward to offer advanced app development possibilities to developers using these technologies.

Finally, another important thing to know is that HTML5 is built upon HTML 4.01, which guarantees backwards compatibility, but adds lots of additional information to the specification, such as:

- Error handling
- Required JavaScript APIs
- Implementation details
- Rendering of HTML5 engines

At the time of this writing, the HTML5 specification has the "Working Draft" status at the W3C.

Declarations and Meta Tags

For those developers used to the quirks and verbosity of HTML, HTML5 is a welcome simplification. Let's see one by one the most important differences for markup developers.

A Minimal HTML5 Document

In its most minimally useful form, an empty HTML5 document looks like this:

```html
<!DOCTYPE html>
<html lang="en">
  <head>
    <meta charset="utf-8">
    <title>title</title>
    <link rel="stylesheet" href="style.css">
    <script src="script.js"></script>
  </head>
  <body>
    <!-- page content -->
  </body>
</html>
```

Let's see in detail the major changes brought by HTML5.

Doctype

This is the most visible change. HTML5 documents must start with this, über-simple DOCTYPE declaration:

```html
<!DOCTYPE html>
```

It could not be any simpler.

Charset

Another welcome simplification is the new charset meta tag; this is what it used to look like:

```html
<meta http-equiv="Content-Type" content="text/html; charset=utf-8">
```

And this is the new version:

```html
<meta charset="utf-8">
```

This should be proof enough that simplicity was a major requirement in the development of HTML5!

JavaScript and Stylesheets

Finally, `<link>` and `<script>` tags are stripped of their "type" parameter, which is not required anymore: ,

```
<link rel="stylesheet" href="style.css">
<script src="app.js">
```

The new HTML5 spec clearly expects style sheets to be CSS files, and scripts to be JavaScript; no more ambiguity here. Oh, and by the way, you do not need to add a closing / to your standalone tags anymore; if you want, you can, but pay attention to the fact that HTML5 *is not based in XHTML*, but in HTML 4.01.

New and Obsolete Elements

Many underused (or downright harmful) tags have been rendered obsolete by HTML5: `<frame>`, `<frameset>`, `<noframes>`, `<acronym>`, `<font>`, `<big>`, `<center>`, `<strike>`. This also includes attributes such as `bgcolor`, `cellspacing`, and `valign`. Just use CSS for them!

The specification also brings new elements to the HTML family: have you heard about `<canvas>`, `<audio>`, `<video>`, `<mark>`, `<time>`, `<meter>`, `<progress>`, `<section>`, `<header>`, or `<article>`? Well, be prepared, as HTML5 will brings definition to the word *web semantics*.

HTML5 Applications

According to the biography by Walter Isaacson, when the first iPhone was released to the public in 2007, Steve Jobs was not fond of the idea of allowing third-party developers write apps for it. He was aiming for a closed platform, where only Apple would deploy its own services, and where external applications would be created using web technologies. As a matter of fact, in the 2007 edition of the WWDC[1] Apple did not introduce a native, official SDK for the iPhone, but rather proposed the idea of building applications using web technologies[2].

As explained at the beginning of this chapter, Apple was one of the "founding fathers" of the original HTML5 specification, together with Opera and the Mozilla Foundation. Many parts of this standard specifically target the use of web technologies as a means to build fully fledged applications, capable of many feats reserved so far to desktop applications:

- Offline storage
- Network connectivity
- Multimedia

---

1. Apple's yearly Worldwide Developers Conference, held in San Francisco.
2. The native SDK would be announced later in October that year, to be finally released in March 2008.

- Sockets and threads
- Drawing and animation
- Advanced form controls

In addition, iPhone pioneered the concept of "adding a web app to the home screen" of the device, allowing users to create bookmarks to their preferred web applications, just like any other app installed in the device.

We are going to see, one by one, the many new features proposed by HTML5 in terms of application development, including sample HTML and JavaScript code for each one of them.

Add Web Apps to Home Screen in iOS

Both iOS and Android allow users to install special bookmarks to web apps on their home screens; this allows users to keep bookmarks to specific web applications, and to access them with a single touch.

In the case of iOS, as shown in Figure 1-1, users can install web applications directly from Safari, by tapping on the action button (in the middle of the toolbar at the bottom of the screen) and then selecting the button labeled "Add to Home Screen," as shown in Figure 1-1.

Figure 1-1. Adding to home screen

Of course, it can be challenging to show this to the user, so thankfully you can use the excellent Add to Home Screen script by Matteo Spinelli (*http://cubiq.org/add-to-home -screen*), which shows a very simple pop-up window, directly on the screen of Safari (on the iPhone, the iPod touch, or the iPad) with the required instructions to perform the operation. This pop up can be configured to appear one or many times, it can be customized to include icons or text, and is also available in many languages! An excellent tool to consider. You can see a screenshot of it in Figure 1-2.

Add Web Apps to Home Screen in Android

In Android devices, adding a web application to the home screen is a bit more difficult, but not impossible:

a. In the browser, add a bookmark for the current page:
   1. Tap the menu button.
   2. Select "Bookmarks."
   3. Select the location marked with a star and the "Add" text.
   4. Tap OK.
b. Tap the "Home" button.
c. On the home screen:
   1. Tap the menu button.
   2. Select "Add."
   3. Select "Shortcut."
   4. Select "Bookmark."
   5. Select the bookmark to your app.

You will have now an icon on your home screen that will take you directly to the web application.

Metadata for HTML5 Applications

You can use the following HTML <meta> and <link> tags in your main HTML file, to specify several features of your application, used by iOS and some of them also by Android, when your application is added to the home screen of your device.

 You can check the complete reference of HTML5 application-related meta tags in the Supported Meta Tags page (*http://developer.apple.com/ library/safari/#documentation/appleapplications/reference/Safar iHTMLRef/Articles/MetaTags.html*) of the Apple Safari Developer Library site.

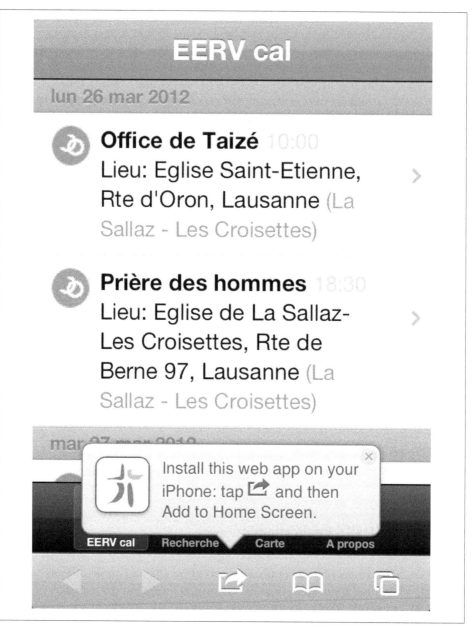

Figure 1-2. The Add to Home script by Matteo Spinelli

The first is the `apple-mobile-web-app-capable` tag; this will allow the application, once it is installed on the home screen of your device, to run on full screen mode, usually called the `standalone` mode. From your own JavaScript code, you can then check whether the application is running in `standalone` mode by checking the `window.naviga` `tor.standalone` property:

```
<meta name="apple-mobile-web-app-capable" content="yes" />
```

Trailing slash or not?

As you can see in the examples in this chapter, HTML5 does not impose trailing slashes at the end of tags, as XHTML would require. Remember that HTML5 is backwards-compatible with HTML 4, and that trailing slashes (or closing tags) are optional (but of course recommended).

The following tag, `viewport`, allows developers to disable the typical pinching and zooming available to users of Mobile Safari:

```
<meta name="viewport" content="initial-scale=1.0, user-scalable=no">
```

The `apple-touch-icon` element specifies the icon to be displayed on the home screen of the device when the HTML5 application is used in standalone mode:

```
<link rel="apple-touch-icon" href="icon.png"/>
```

You can also specify several different sizes and resolutions, to be used on different devices:

```
<link rel="apple-touch-icon" sizes="72x72" href="touch-icon-ipad.png" />
<link rel="apple-touch-icon" sizes="114x114" href="touch-icon-iphone4.png" />
```

The files referenced in the `apple-touch-icon` tag must have the sizes explained in the Technical Q&A QA1686 by Apple (*http://developer.apple.com/library/ios/#qa/qa1686/_index.html*), which specifies all the possible icon sizes for iOS application, including those required in devices with Retina displays, such as the iPhone 4, the iPhone 4S, or the new iPad released in 2012. If no size is specified, then the file must be 57 pixels in width and height.

For the complete reference of file names for web app icons, check the Configuring web applications (*http://developer.apple.com/library/ios/#DOCUMENTATION/AppleApplications/Reference/SafariWebContent/ConfiguringWebApplications/ConfiguringWebApplications.html*) section in the iOS Developer Library from Apple.

By default, the icon specified for the standalone application will feature a glare effect, applied automatically by iOS; if you do not want to have that effect, because your designer has already applied some visual pizazz to your icon, you can do two different things:

1. You can name your file *apple-touch-icon-precomposed.png*.

2. You can use the `rel="apple-touch-icon-precomposed"` attribute in your `link` tag, as shown in the following code snippet:

```
<link rel="apple-touch-icon-precomposed" href="icon.png"/>
```

Another useful tag allows developers to change the look and feel of the status bar, shown on top of every iPhone application; this status bar can be changed only when your HTML file already contains the `apple-mobile-web-app-capable` tag, and when it is running on `standalone` mode:

```
<meta name="apple-mobile-web-app-status-bar-style" content="black">
```

The final element, `apple-touch-startup-image` specifies a file that is shown by iOS when the web application is starting. This is a visual trick that creates the illusion of the application starting up faster than it really does.

 The file referenced by the `apple-touch-startup-image` tag must have exactly 320 x 460 pixels. If the file has a different size, it will not be shown by the system.

```
<link rel="apple-touch-startup-image" href="Default.png" />
```

HTML5 Application Cache

In their most simple nature, mobile web applications require a network connection to offer their services. The world, however, is far from an ideal place, and we all know that network connections are shaky at best. Tunnels, big buildings, airplanes, elevators, trains, and the countryside are all typical environments where our smartphones are cut off from the network. We need, however, to be able to use our applications in those situations as well, and this is why working offline is one of the most important requirements for mobile apps.

The ability of a web application to work offline is a big feature of HTML5. HTML5 uses the newly introduced *cache manifest* feature[3] to list the resources to fetch while connected to server and maintain while to be used while offline.

HTML5 cache manifests are simple text files, specifying the list of files that have to be kept in the browser after they have been requested. They can also contain references to files or URLs that cannot be kept offline (for technical or legal reasons), and the mobile browser uses this information to speed up the rendering of the application.

Let's take a look at a simple cache manifest, taken from an application written by the author of this book:

```
CACHE MANIFEST
# version 7
```

---

3. The official documentation of the HTML5 application cache is available at the W3C site (*http://www.w3 .org/TR/html5/offline.html*).

```
CACHE:
index.html
icon.png
app.js
style.css
/_libs/sencha/sencha-touch.js
/_libs/sencha/resources/css/sencha-touch.css

NETWORK:
http://maps.gstatic.com/
http://maps.google.com/
http://maps.googleapis.com/
http://mt0.googleapis.com/
http://mt1.googleapis.com/
http://mt2.googleapis.com/
http://mt3.googleapis.com/
http://khm0.googleapis.com/
http://khm1.googleapis.com/
http://cbk0.googleapis.com/
http://cbk1.googleapis.com/
http://www.google-analytics.com/
http://gg.google.com/
http://google-maps-utility-library-v3.googlecode.com/

FALLBACK:
offline.html
```

The application cache is simply a text file (encoded in UTF-8) that consists of major sections:

A CACHE *section*
> This part specifies the relative and/or absolute URLs of the resources that the device should keep offline.

A NETWORK *section*
> This part of the application cache lists the URLs of the resources that cannot (or must not) be kept offline. For example, in this case (a real cache manifest from an application written by the author) we are specifying all the URLs of the Google Maps API (*https://developers.google.com/maps/*), which, according to Google's Terms of Service, cannot be cached offline.

A FALLBACK *section*
> This section provides a URL that will be served whenever a resource specified in the NETWORK section is required when the application is offline.

Once your application cache manifest file is defined, you can use it in your HTML files as follows:

```
<!DOCTYPE html>
<html lang="en" manifest="app.manifest">  <!-- ❶ -->
  <head>
    <meta charset="utf-8">
    <title>title</title>
    <link rel="stylesheet" href="style.css">
    <script src="script.js"></script>
```

```
    </head>
    <body>
      <!-- page content -->
    </body>
  </html>
```

❶ Here we are specifying the application cache manifest file that belongs to this HTML file.

According to Maximiliano Firtman's Mobile HTML5 site (*http://mobilehtml5.org/*), shown in Figure 1-3, the HTML5 application cache is supported by most major mobile platforms today.

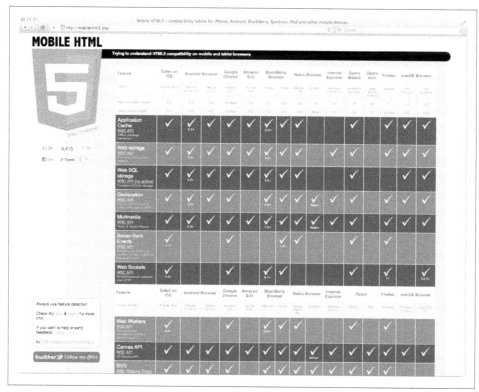

Figure 1-3. Mobile HTML5 site by Maximiliano Firtman

Cache manifests are very flexible, but they have one important restrictions; to be recognized as such, they *must* be served with the `text/cache-manifest` MIME type. In the following sections, you'll learn how to configure some popular web server platforms and technologies, in order to serve HTML5 Application Cache manifests properly.

The HTML5 Application Cache is a very interesting technology, but it also has several quirks and gotchas that are not always easy to spot or to debug. Please read the article "Application Cache is a Douchebag" (*http://www.alistapart.com/articles/application-cache-is-a-douche bag/*) in A List Apart, which provides excellent details about all the potential problems, and how to solve them.

Manifest Files in Apache

For example, in Apache, you can use the following line in your local *.htaccess* file to force all files ending with the `.manifest` extension to be served with this MIME type:

```
AddType text/cache-manifest .manifest
```

Manifest Files with PHP

A very simple technique to return HTML5 application cache manifests is to create a short PHP file (in this case, named *manifest.php*) with the following contents:

```
<?php
header("Content-Type: text/cache-manifest");
?>
CACHE MANIFEST
# version 7

CACHE:
index.html
icon.png
app.js
...
```

As you can see, using the `header` function we can set the proper MIME type. To use this manifest, just place this attribute in your HTML file:

```
<html manifest="manifest.php">
```

However, be aware that some older versions of iOS actually expect the HTML5 manifest to have the `.manifest` extension to work, even if the file is returned with the proper MIME type. As usual, testing is required!

Manifest Files in IIS

To deliver HTML5 manifest files from servers running Windows 7, Windows Server 2008, Windows Server 2008 R2, or Windows Vista with IIS, you can define new MIME types in your server following these steps:

1. Open the IIS manager.
2. In the "Features" view, select "MIME types."
3. In the "Actions" panel, select "Add."

4. The "Add MIME Type" dialog box appears; type the .manifest file extension; in the corresponding text field.

5. Enter the following MIME type in the other text box: "text/cache-manifest."

6. Click OK.

7. Restart IIS and you are done.

For more information, including command-line actions for doing this, check out the Microsoft Technet site (*http://technet.microsoft.com/en-us/library/cc725608(v=ws.10) .aspx*).

Manifest Files in .NET

If you do not want (or cannot) modify the configuration of your web server, you can define custom MIME types directly in `.config` files. For that, you can create a `Web.con fig` file with the following contents[4]:

```xml
<?xml version="1.0"?>
<configuration>
    <system.webServer>
        <staticContent>
            <remove fileExtension=".manifest"/>
            <mimeMap fileExtension=".manifest" mimeType="text/cache-manifest"/>
        </staticContent>
    </system.webServer>
</configuration>
```

Another option, explained by Stephen Walther in his blog (*http://stephenwalther.com/ blog/archive/2011/01/26/creating-html5-offline-web-applications-with-asp-net.aspx*), consists in a custom handler (named `Manifest.ashx` in this example) that sets the proper MIME type and outputs the contents of a text file:

```csharp
using System.Web;

namespace JavaScriptReference {
    public class Manifest : IHttpHandler {
        public void ProcessRequest(HttpContext context) {
            context.Response.ContentType = "text/cache-manifest";
            context.Response.WriteFile(context.Server.MapPath("Manifest.txt"));
        }

        public bool IsReusable {
            get {
                return false;
            }
        }
    }
}
```

---

4. This is explained by James Skemp in his blog post (*http://strivinglife.com/words/post/Supporting-HTML5 -manifest-files-on-IIS-7-using-Webconfig.aspx*).

Then, from your HTML5 file, you need to reference the URL of the handler configured in your ASP.NET application:

```
<html manifest="Manifest.ashx">
```

This option is a bit more complex, but it might prove useful as a way to automatically create manifest files, reading the contents of folders and such.

Debugging Manifest Files

As cool as HTML5 application manifests are, they are quite tricky to troubleshoot and debug; there are, however, a couple of tricks that are useful and that every mobile web developer should keep in mind while working with them:

- Some versions of iOS 4 not only expect your manifest files to have the `text/cache-manifest` MIME type, they also expect the file to have the `.manifest` extension; if your application is not caching data properly in older versions of iOS, remember to rename your manifest file accordingly.

- To force a refresh of the local cache, you have to update the manifest file; however, this happens only when the actual contents of the file have changed (that is, you cannot just `touch` the file to trigger the change). The easiest way is then to add a `version` line (seen in the example at the beginning of this section) which can be augmented whenever required, even if the actual contents of the file are not changed.

- In iOS 5, it is very easy to remove all files from the offline application cache; just open the Settings application on your device, select the Safari settings, scroll to the bottom, and select the "Advanced" entry; in that section you will see a "Website Data" entry, where you can see the amount of data stored by each website you visited on your device. Clicking the "Edit" button helps you remove individual entries; you can also remove all website data just by using the "Clear Cookies and Data" button in the main Safari settings.

Testing for HTML5 Features

Given the tremendous array of HTML5 technologies in place, a valid question would be, "How can I be sure that feature xyz is available in this particular combination of operating system and browser?" To answer this question, you could take the long road and check a site such as Mobile HTML5 (*http://mobilehtml5.org/*) by Maximiliano Firtman, and start writing lots of spaghetti-like `if` & `else` statements all over the place.

Please, do not do this[5]. The recommended technique for any kind of HTML5 application these days is *feature detection*. In this approach, you do not care about the specifics

---

5. I mean, of course check Maximiliano's site, but do not write spaghetti code!

of a particular operating system or browser version; just ask the browser (whichever it is) *for a particular feature*, and you are done.

Even better, there is a library that does this for you: Modernizr (*http://www.modernizr .com/*) provides a cross-platform library that exposes a simple, useful `Modernizr` global variable, where you can ask for a number of features in your JavaScript code:

```
if (Modernizr.geolocation) {
    // this browser supports geolocation
}

if (Modernizr.touch) {
    // this is a touchscreen-enabled browser
}
else {
    // no touchscreen, so you should use the common mouse interactions
}
```

The number of properties exposed by the `Modernizr` object is outstanding: `fontface`, `opacity`, `cssanimations`, `applicationcache`, `localstorage`, `webgl`... and the list goes on. Check the Modernizr documentation (*http://www.modernizr.com/docs/*) for more information about all the possibilities offered by this library.

Even better, when you use Modernizr in older browsers without HTML5 features (think IE6), it will load what it calls "polyfills," that is, small bits of JavaScript which will provide the same interface as their HTML5 counterparts! This way you can create just one application, using as many HTML5 features as required, and your code will work gracefully in older or newer versions of your favorite browser.

Modernizr supports IE6+, Firefox 3.5+, Opera 9.6+, Safari 2+, Google Chrome mobile, Mobile Safari on iOS, Android's browser, Opera Mobile, Firefox Mobile, and (still under development at the time of this writing) Blackberry 6+. You can create a production-ready Modernizr script, only with the features that you need, from the Modernizr download page (*http://www.modernizr.com/download/*).

We are going to use Modernizr in the following sections of this chapter, to test for the existence of the features we are going to talk about.

Geolocation

One of the new possibilities offered by HTML5 is being able to access the geolocation data from within a web application. There is a very simple JavaScript API that allows you to do this:

```
function success(position) {
    // Did we get the position correctly?
    console.log(position.coords.latitude);
}

function error(error) {
    switch(error.code) {
```

```
        case error.TIMEOUT:
            console.log('Timeout');
            break;

        case error.POSITION_UNAVAILABLE:
            console.log('Position unavailable');
            break;

        case error.PERMISSION_DENIED:
            console.log('Permission denied');
            break;

        case error.UNKNOWN_ERROR:
            console.log('Unknown error');
            break;
    }
}

if (Modernizr.geolocation) {
    navigator.geolocation.getCurrentPosition(success, error);
}
```

For privacy reasons, the browser will ask the user permission to use this information. Coupled with the Google Maps API, you can create compelling geolocation-enabled application directly from your browser.

Device Orientation

Another cool element of the HTML5 umbrella is the device orientation API. This API allows you to detect the position of the orientation of the device in space, and to redraw your user interface accordingly:

```
function handleOrientation(eventData) {
    // alpha is the compass direction the device is facing in degrees
    var alpha = eventData.alpha;

    // gamma is the left-to-right tilt in degrees, where right is positive
    var gamma = eventData.gamma;

    // beta is the front-to-back tilt in degrees, where front is positive
    var beta = eventData.beta;

    var data = [alpha, beta, gamma];

    console.log('Orientation changed: ' + data.join(', '));
}

if (Modernizr.deviceorientation) {
    window.addEventListener('deviceorientation', handleOrientation, false);
}
```

The device orientation event returns only the rotation data, which includes how much the device is leaning side-to-side (beta), front-to-back (gamma), and if the phone or laptop has a compass, the direction the device is facing (alpha).

Device Motion

Similar to the orientation API, the device motion API of HTML5 returns information about the acceleration of the current device. Acceleration data is returned as a coordinate frame with three axes, x, y, and z. The x-axis runs side-to-side across the mobile phone screen and is positive towards the right side. The y-axis runs front-to-back across the mobile phone screen and is positive towards as it moves away from you. The z-axis comes straight up out of the mobile phone screen and is positive as it moves up.

The device motion event is a superset of the device orientation event. It returns data about the rotation information and also acceleration information about the device. The acceleration data is returned in three axes: x, y, and z. They are measured in meters per second squared (m/s^2). Because some devices might not have the hardware to exclude the effect of gravity, the event returns two properties, `accelerationIncludingGravity` and `acceleration`, which excludes the effects of gravity (when this is the case, the acceleration data will be null):

```
function handleDeviceMotion(eventData) {
    // Grab the acceleration including gravity from the results
    var acc = eventData.accelerationIncludingGravity;
    var accData = [
        Math.round(acc.x),
        Math.round(acc.y),
        Math.round(acc.z)
    ];

    // Display the raw acceleration data
    var rawAcc = "[" + accData.join(", ") + "]";

    // Z is the acceleration in the Z axis, and tells us if the device is facing up,
or down
    var facingUp = -1;
    if (acc.z > 0) {
        facingUp = +1;
    }

    // Convert the value from acceleration to degress
    // acc.x|y is the acceleration according to gravity, we'll assume we're on Earth
and divide
    // by 9.81 (earth gravity) to get a percentage value, and then multiply that by 90
to convert to degrees.
    var tiltLR = Math.round(((acc.x) / 9.81) * -90);
    var tiltFB = Math.round(((acc.y + 9.81) / 9.81) * 90 * facingUp);
    var tilt = [tiltLR, tiltFB];

    console.log('Acceleration: ' + rawAcc);
    console.log('Facing up? ' + facingUp);
```

```
        console.log('Tilt: ' + tilt.join(', '));
    }

    if (Modernizr.devicemotion) {
        window.addEventListener('devicemotion', handleDeviceMotion, false);
    }
```

Network Connectivity

Mobile web applications storing their resources offline might need to know whether the device is online or not, for example to update their information, ping a remote server or provide some supplementary service. To do that, HTML5 introduces a small yet very useful API: the network connectivity API.

```
    function deviceOnline(e) {
        console.log('device is online');
    }

    function deviceOffline(e) {
        console.log('device is offline');
    }

    if (Modernizr.applicationcache) {
        window.addEventListener("online", deviceOnline, false);
        window.addEventListener("offline", deviceOffline, false);
    }
```

The new online and offline events are triggered whenever the connectivity status of the current device changes, allowing the developer to perform some operation in that moment.

The network connectivity API also provides an imperative way to ask the current device whether the device is connected or not:

```
    if (Modernizr.applicationcache) {
        if (navigator.onLine) {
            console.log('This device is online');
        }
        else {
            console.log('This device is offline');
        }
    }
```

Pay attention to the fact that the event is spelled online while the property on the navigator object is spelled onLine... this is a common source of errors.

Network connectivity = Internet access

You must be aware that this API is not reliable; your device might be connected to a network, yet not have a proper Internet access. For example, routers could be down, you could have a self-assigned IP address, and many other situations could provide a "false positive" in the API calls above. In those cases, you should always provide error callbacks to your XMLHttpRequest calls, so that you are able to fail gracefully in some situations.

This API is a perfect companion for the HTML5 Application Manifest; taking your application offline and being able to tell (with certain accuracy) whether you are online or not, can help you create more sophisticated applications covering different and complex use cases.

Canvas

The new <canvas> object is, together with CSS3 animations, one of the few HTML5 features that are available in nearly all modern browsers at the time of this writing[6].

The Canvas API allows developers to perform 2D drawing on a section of the web page; this section, conveniently called the canvas, is implemented through the new <canvas> object, originally introduced in the WebKit project by Apple.

To use the Canvas API you have to first define a <canvas> element in your HTML file:

```
<canvas id="canvasObject" width="320" height="480">
Any text displayed here will be used as fallback, in case the current browser
does not support the canvas object.
</canvas>
```

Once this is in place, the rest happens in JavaScript code:

```
if (Modernizr.canvas) {
    var canvasObject = document.getElementById('canvasObject'); ❶

    if (canvasObject) {
        var context = canvasObject.getContext('2d'); ❷
        if (context) {
            context.fillRect(0, 0, 150, 100); ❸

            // This sample comes from
            // http://dev.opera.com/articles/view/html-5-canvas-the-basics/
            context.fillStyle   = '#00f'; // blue
            context.strokeStyle = '#f00'; // red
            context.lineWidth   = 4;

            // Draw some rectangles.
            context.fillRect  (0,   0, 150, 50);
            context.strokeRect(0,  60, 150, 50);
```

6. Source: Mobile HTML5 by Maximiliano Firtman (*http://mobilehtml5.org/*)

```
                    // Draw an image
                    var image = new Image();
                    image.src = "http://someserver.com/somepath/file.gif"
                    image.onload = function () {
                        // Loading an image can take a while; hence the callback on the onload
                        // event... which is executed asynchronously.
                        context.drawImage(image, 10, 40);
                    }
                }
            }
        }
```

❶ Here we retrieve a pointer to the <canvas> element in our HTML file, defined in the previous snippet.

❷ Here we get a reference to the 2D drawing context of the <canvas> element; there are apparently plans to provide a 3D context one day, but there are no standard or complete implementations available yet.

❸ ... and from here on we actually draw something!

The most important thing to know about the Canvas drawing API is that it is a stateful API, whose design is based on a real painter canvas, where every paint stroke goes on top of the previous one. The Canvas API provides functions that allows developers to draw the following primitives:

- Rectangles
- Ellipses (and circles, of course)
- Arbitrary lines and paths, with any stroke width and color
- Arbitrary images, loaded from any URL
- Text
- Gradients

Finally, the <canvas> object also exposes a .toDataURL method, which takes a MIME type as parameter, allowing the end user to export any drawing to another format:

```
if (Modernizr.datauri) {
    var url = canvas.toDataURL("image/png");
    window.open(url);
}
```

The code above works in some mobile browsers that understand special URLs starting with the data:image/gif;base64,R0lGODlhyAD3APcAAAA... text, which allows images to be inlined using their base64 representation. This works in most recent smartphone browsers, like Safari on iOS and the Android browser, and thankfully Modernizr provides a datauri test that allows us to wrap the code properly, and eventually to provide a fallback solution.

A Tool for Generating Canvas Drawings

There is a very interesting tool for the Mac, that can be used to draw complex illustrations, and to export them as <canvas> code: Opacity (*http://likethought.com/opacity/*). This commercial tool allows to export any drawing (within limitation) as JavaScript code targeting the <canvas> object, so you and your design team might want to check it out.

CSS3 Animations and Transitions

In October 2007 (*http://www.webkit.org/blog/138/css-animation/*) the WebKit browser engine included for the first time the capability to animate effects using CSS properties. These properties were lated introduced in the CSS3 standard, which is commonly considered part of the overall HTML5 technology umbrella.

Why are animations and transitions a part of CSS and not, say, JavaScript functions or objects [7]? It turns out that considering them as presentational rather than behavioral parts of a web page has several advantages:

- It allows to separate animation and transitions from other JavaScript behaviors, which basically simplifies the development of applications.
- CSS animations and transitions can be hardware-accelerated, by executing them in the GPU rather than in the CPU of your device; this is even more important in relatively low powered mobile devices.

Familiar to Core Animation and Flash developers

The specification of CSS3 animations and transitions will appear very familiar to iOS and Adobe Flash developers; concepts like timing functions, keyframes, animatable properties and other keywords will resonate in those developers having experience with iOS and OS X Core Animation framework, as well as in those who have been exposed to Flash movies and animations.

Transitions

You can think of transitions as simple animations, that occur when certain values of some CSS property is changed.

The simplest possible transition can be achieved with the following CSS code:

---

7. Actually, the whole "Animations are presentation or behavior" debate was fueled by long discussions about the relative merits of both approaches to the same problem; for example, Jonathan Snook first expressed concern and disagreement about considering animations and transitions as presentation (*http://snook.ca/archives/javascript/css_animations_in_safari/*) and later changed his mind. (*http://snook.ca/archives/html_and_css/shifting-opinion-css-animations*)

```
li.animatedHover {
    -webkit-transition-property: background-color, color;
    -webkit-transition-duration: 500ms;
    -moz-transition-property: background-color, color;
    -moz-transition-duration: 500ms;
    -o-transition-property: background-color, color;
    -o-transition-duration: 500ms;
    -ms-transition-property: background-color, color;
    -ms-transition-duration: 500ms;
    transition-property: background-color, color;
    transition-duration: 500ms;
    background-color: green;
    color: white;
}

li.animatedHover:hover {
    background-color: yellow;
    color: black;
}
```

 As you can see, unfortunately we have to specify the individual prefixes for all browser vendors (like -webkit, -moz, etc) to make sure that these transitions are enabled in most browsers. You might want to use a language like SASS (*http://sass-lang.com/*) or LESS (*http://lesscss.org/*) to remove duplication and to streamline the generation of your CSS stylesheets.

The above CSS styles can be used in any `<li>` element that has the `animatedHover` class:

```
<ol>
    <li class="animatedHover">First</li>
    <li class="animatedHover">Second</li>
    <li class="animatedHover">Third</li>
    <li class="animatedHover">Fourth</li>
    <li class="animatedHover">Fifth</li>
</ol>
```

If you move your mouse over any of these elements, you are going to see that the transition between green and yellow is animated; the following CSS properties are used:

- `transition-property` instruction in the CSS file specifies which properties to animate. You can use the `all` keyword to indicate that all properties should be considered for an animation, but this should be used with care.

- `transition-duration` specifies the duration of the operation [8]

- `transition-delay` can be used to introduce a certain time (specified in `ms` or `s`) before the transition is triggered.

- `transition-timing-function` specifies the acceleration pattern of the animation:

---

8. In this case, in milliseconds, but you can also specify `s` to specify a time in seconds; this is part of the CSS3 standard.

- ease, which is the default value.
- linear, which specifies no acceleration at all.
- ease-in, which specifies acceleration only when the animation starts.
- ease-out, which specifies acceleration only when the animation stops.
- ease-in-out, which specifies acceleration at the beginning and a deceleration at the end of the animation.

Animations

Animations are very similar to transitions, but they introduce some complexity of their own. To begin with, they also allow developers to define transitions between values of specific CSS properties; you can use all the properties that you commonly use for transitions.

However, they also provide the capacity of specifying keyframes, which should be familiar to developers having experience with Adobe Flash. Animations can also be repeated a certain number of times, and they can also be played backwards.

Let's implement a simple animation; let's consider a square, red <div id="animated Block"></div> element in our page, with a bit of CSS to animate it around the page.

```
#animatedBlock {
    height: 100px;
    width: 100px;
    display: block;
    position: absolute;
    top: 200px;
    left: 200px;
    background-color: red;
}
```

(This is not a book about design, which means that I can draw extremely ugly boxes to demonstrate concepts!) Now let's define an animation to our block:

```
#animatedBlock {
    height: 100px;
    width: 100px;
    display: block;
    position: absolute;
    top: 200px;
    left: 200px;
    background-color: red;

    -webkit-animation-delay: 300ms;
    -webkit-animation-name: pulsating-animation; ❶
    -webkit-animation-duration: 10s;
    -webkit-animation-iteration-count: infinite; ❷
    -webkit-animation-timing-function: ease-in;
    -webkit-animation-direction: normal;
    -webkit-animation-play-state: running; ❸
    -webkit-animation-direction: alternate; ❹
```

```
    }

    @-webkit-keyframes pulsating-animation
    {
        0% {
            height: 100px;
            width: 100px;
        }

        100%
        {
            height: 300px;
            width: 300px;
        }
    }
```

❶ Very important: *Do not quote this value!* The animation name is used as is, and of course you can specify any kind of name.

❷ The `infinite` value specifies that the animation will never stop (at least, not until the `animation-play-state` property is set to `paused`).

❸ The `animation-play-state` property can also be set to `paused` to stop the animation. This can be done using JavaScript code as well.

❹ If `animation-direction` is set to `normal` then the animation jumps back to the default position at start without animation. The `alternate` keyword makes the animation return to the default state with an animation played backwards.

The example above will make the `<div>` element grow in size, back and forth, from 100 pixels to 300 pixels in 10 seconds. This will be repeated forever, with a timing function that accelerates the movement when the animation starts, and where the same animation is played backwards before repeating itself.

The `@-webkit-keyframes` section defines, for the animation named `pulsating-anima tion`, the different values of the animatable properties taken into account in this sequence; the browser takes this information to interpolate the intermediate values to provide the final animation on the page.

Final Considerations

Before you start using CSS3 transitions and animations in your sites and applications, you might want to remember the following facts:

- It is important to know which properties can be animated: the official W3C page for CSS Transitions (*http://www.w3.org/TR/css3-transitions/#animatable-proper ties-*) provides an extensive list of properties that are "animatable"; for example, beyond the `background-color` and `color` properties we have just seen, the following properties are also animatable: `border-color` `font-size`, `height`, `opacity`, `text-`

`shadow`, `z-index`, `left`, `top`, `right`, `bottom`, `margin`, and `padding` (including all of their flavors).

- Beware of usability, accessibility and health issues related with animations on a computer screen; the fact that you are *able* to animate elements does not mean that you *should* do it.
- Nearly all modern mobile browsers support CSS3 transitions and animations; Internet Explorer 10 (at least in its developer previews), Firefox since version 5, Safari since 4, Chrome since 9, Opera since 10.6 [9], iOS since 3.2 and Android since 2.1.

Client-Side Storage

One of the most exciting new features about HTML5 is the set of new specifications that enables client-side storage options for HTML5 web applications. Web Storage is a very simple API, composed of two different global objects that can store and retrieve strings:

- localStorage is persisted even if the user closes the browser
- sessionStorage is not persisted, and is removed when the user closes the browser window

These two objects act as global dictionaries, that can be populated and queried using any key (which must be a string, too):

```
if (Modernizr.localstorage) {
    // Just append key values to this dictionary!
    // It's that easy. However only strings are supported!
    localStorage.someData = "some data here";

    // You can also use the common 'dictionary' syntax
    localStorage['some complex key'] = 'some complex data there';
}

if (Modernizr.sessionstorage) {
    // This data will only persist while the current
    // browser window is open!
    sessionStorage.someData = "some data here";

    // Similarly, you can also use the 'dictionary' syntax:
    sessionStorage['just keep this for now'] = true;
}
```

HTML5 web applications are able to store up to 5 MB of data in the local browser, which is usually more than enough for mobile applications. In some particular cases, though, applications might require users to store more than 5 MB. For those cases, iOS provides developers with a bonus feature. Your application can continue storing data

---

9. At the time of this writing, Opera supports only transitions, not animations, but apparently they will be supported in version 12, currently in beta.

Figure 1-4. Financial Times web application requesting more data

until it reaches the limit of 5 MB, and when it goes beyond that limit, Safari will ask the user for extending the maximum. You can see this mechanism in action when opening the Financial Times Web Application (*http://apps.ft.com/ftwebapp/*) on an iPad, as shown in Figure 1-4.

 In the case of SQL Storage (described in the following section), the maximum limit can be set to 50 MB, as described in this StackOverflow question (*http://stackoverflow.com/a/6281947/133764:*).

Developers can use the web inspector included in WebKit-based browsers, such as Safari and Chrome, to inspect and modify the contents of the localStorage and ses sionStorage objects, as shown in Figure 1-5.

SQL Storage

Once part of the original HTML5 specification, the Web SQL Database is a very im‐ pressive piece of technology, allowing you to create, update, and edit items stored in a local SQL database on the browser. Similar to localStorage items, web SQL databases allow you to persist structured data in your browser, allowing developers to use the full power of the SQLite database engine (*http://sqlite.org/*) embedded in most mobile browsers these days.

The code below shows a snippet of code, required to create a new database, and to execute a transactional SQL statement. The API is asynchronous, and requires the

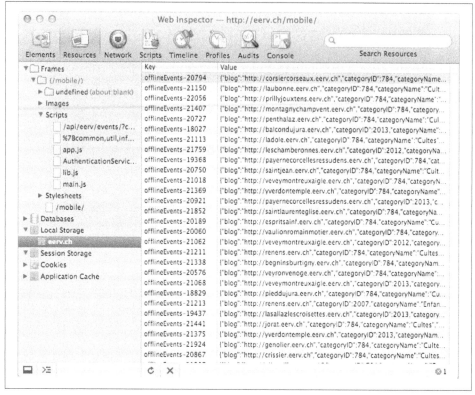

Figure 1-5. Inspecting the local storage in the WebKit inspector

developer to specify a callback function to be executed once the SQL operations are completed:

```
this.db = openDatabase('geomood', '1.0', 'Geo-Mood Checkins', 8192);
this.db.transaction(function(tx) {
    tx.executeSql("create table if not exists " +
            "checkins(id integer primary key asc, time integer, latitude float," +
                    "longitude float, mood string)",
            [],
            function() { console.log("done"); }
    );
});
```

Even if many modern mobile browsers support this feature, unfortunately the W3C Web Application Working Group no longer maintains it (*http://www.w3.org/TR/web database/*), and some consider this API as deprecated. The proposed replacement is the IndexedDB API (*http://www.w3.org/TR/IndexedDB/*) which is (at the time of this writing) only supported by Google Chrome for Android and Firefox (*http://caniuse.com/ indexeddb*). In any case, a good rule of thumb is to ignore this otherwise excellent idea.

Rich Media Tags

Probably the most hyped feature of HTML5 are the new media elements `<canvas>`, `<video>`, and `<audio>`. They have been tailored to bring native media functionality to the browser *without the need for a plug-in* (which usually was Adobe Flash).

Not all is perfect, though, as different browser vendors still do not support the same media formats, and care must be taken to ensure that all HTML5-compliant browsers can play the same audio and video. This usually can be done by nesting different formats in the same `<audio>` tag:

```
<audio>
    <source src="audio.ogg">
    <source src="audio.mp3">
</audio>
```

To solve these incompatibilities in the case of video, solutions such as SublimeVideo (*http://sublimevideo.net/*), created by the Swiss company Jilion (*http://jilion.com*), allow web developers to use a cross-browser HTML5 player in their applications.

Conclusion

HTML5 is a breakthrough specification in terms of simplicity, extensibility, and focus on applications. It is strongly suggested to start using HTML5 documents in all your applications, and do not forget to validate them using the excellent HTML5 Validator (*http://validator.nu/*) by Henri Sivonen!

CHAPTER 2

JavaScript Productivity Tips

This chapter will provide some basic syntax elements about JavaScript, just to get all readers to the same level. If you are comfortable with advanced JavaScript idioms, feel free to skip this chapter altogether. We are going to use the examples in this chapter to "stretch our legs" and get comfortable with the language[1].

Not for Beginners

This chapter is meant for developers familiar with the basics of Java-Script; it will not go through all the features of the language, but in particular over those that really make a difference when writing a large JavaScript application. And, of course, the criteria for choosing those features is entirely under the highly subjective perspective of the author of this book!

About JavaScript

JavaScript is the world's most misunderstood language (*http://www.crockford.com/javascript/javascript.html*), which means that, as Yoda would say, you must unlearn what you have learned (*http://www.imdb.com/title/tt0080684/quotes?qt=qt0358473*). However complicated it might seem at first, it is quite easy to write and understand the most complex of JavaScript codes with just some examples.

This page (*http://developer.mozilla.org/en/docs/A_re-introduction_to_JavaScript*) provides an excellent complement of information to know JavaScript better, as well as the Wikipedia page (*http://en.wikipedia.org/wiki/JavaScript*).

---

1. The code samples in this chapter are adapted from a series of articles in the Open Kosmaczewski blog (*http://kosmaczewski.net/javascript-tips-tricks-2/*) by the author of this book.

Some Coding Tips

When you are writing JavaScript code, the following tips might be of help:

- In JavaScript, all the properties of an object are public, virtual, and overridable; that means that you can override the default implementation of any method on any object, or on any "class," and provide your own implementation; this is, as you can imagine, great and terrible at the same time.

- Always add semicolons at the end of your statements; they are not mandatory, but they are strongly recommended. In this book, all code examples use semicolons.

- Always write the closing bracket whenever you open one; JavaScript expressions can have lots of embedded curly, round, and square brackets, and closing them as soon as you open them will save you lots of debugging hours.

- Always use the "var" keyword when defining variables. Otherwise, the variables will be created on the "Global Object" of JavaScript, and this is a bad thing for two reasons:

  1. Variables created in the "Global Object" *are not garbage collected in some browsers!*

  2. *You are polluting the global namespace!* If you use a variable called `location` in your code, and you forget to use the `var` keyword, your variable will be defined in the global namespace and will override the standard `location` object... which is not a good idea, for all the reasons you can imagine!

- The default return value of JavaScript function (that is, when there is not a `return` statement) is `undefined`. Is not `null`, but `undefined`. This is a very important thing to remember when debugging code.

- Validate your JavaScript code with JSLint (*http://jslint.com/*). JSLint can also be installed locally in your development machine, and some editors like Vim (*http://www.vim.org/*) allow to automatically execute JSLint when you save JavaScript files (in the case of Vim, that's thanks to the jslint.vim (*http://www.vim.org/scripts/script.php?script_id=2729*) or the javascriptlint.vim (*http://github.com/joestelmach/javaScriptLint.vim*) plug-ins).

Object Literals

First of all, every object in JavaScript is a map (or hash), and you can access properties and methods using either the `dot.syntax` or the `["array"]` syntax:

```
var obj = {
    age: 42,
    "first and last name": "John Smith", // yes, you can do that
    address: {
        street: "32 Kingston St.",
        city: "Springfield",
        zip: 12345
```

```
        },
        greet: function() {
            console.log('hello! my name is ' +
            this["first and last name"] + ' and my age is ' + this.age.toString());
        }
    };

    console.log(obj["first and last name"]); // shows "John Smith"
    console.log(obj.age === obj["age"]); // shows "true" ('===' is the identity operator)
    console.log(typeof obj); // shows "object"
    obj.greet();
```

Since the `dot.syntax` and the `["array"]` syntaxes are equivalent, you must by now imagine that every "dot" in your code means a search into a dictionary (or literal object). *So, the fewer "dots" you use when calling an object, function or expression, the faster it is!*

To achieve this, use shortcuts:

```
    var a = {
        very: {
            interesting: {
                JavaScript: {
                    object: {
                        reference: "longer than needed, but it's just an example!"
                    }
                }
            }
        }
    };

    var shortcut = a.very.interesting.JavaScript.object.reference;
    console.log(shortcut);
```

Single or Double Quotes?

I regularly teach these concepts to developers all over the world, yet the same question always pops up: strings in JavaScript, double or single quotes?

It turns out that both are interchangeable; you can use either as you want. However, certain rules and protocols apply:

- You can create strings using either apostrophes or quotes. You can also *mix them* as you want, but always keep the nesting order when using them.
- In general, it is considered good practice and style to use single quotes whenever possible. This is particularly useful when JavaScript has to manipulate HTML strings, where double quotes are considered the standard:

```
    var singleQuoted = 'single quoted string';
    var doubleQuoted = "double quoted string";

    // External single quotes are preferred in general, by convention
    var html = '<p class="header">This is some HTML snippet</p>';
```

JavaScript Base Types

JavaScript is an object-oriented language without classes; the language standard defines, however, seven core object types, that could be assimilated to classes in other languages, and that are actually referred to as classes sometimes in the literature.

The following are the seven core JavaScript types that are part of the ECMA standard:

- Object (root type, like in Java)
- String
- Number
- Array
- Date
- RegExp
- Function

For a handy reference of the core JavaScript API, download and print this cheat sheet (*http://www.addedbytes.com/cheat-sheets/javascript-cheat-sheet/*).

The types enumerated above are always present, in all JavaScript implementations (Adobe Flash ActionScript, Microsoft JScript, ECMAScript, etc.).

When JavaScript runs in a web browser, other types and objects are added, like Window, Document, and others. These objects are part of the *DOM* (Document Object Model) and are browser-specific (and based on W3C standards).

Dynamic Overloading of Base Types

It is important to know that, since JavaScript is a dynamic language, that Functions are used as classes, are fully fledged objects, and that you can *add methods to a class on the fly*, usually called (dynamic overloading):

```
String.prototype.doSomething = function() {
  console.log(this);
}

"hello!".doSomething();
```

This behavior is simple to understand, and will be familiar to developers who have used Python, Ruby, or Objective-C in the past.

Functions

Functions are the basic block in JavaScript. You use them everywhere, you can pass them as parameters, attach them as event handlers, override them, delete them, etc. Functions can be anonymous or not:

```
// In the example below, dont forget the semicolon!
// However, its name will not appear in the debugger
var anonymous = function() {
    console.log('anonymous function!');
};

// This the classic syntax, without a semicolon at the end!
function nonAnonymous() {
    console.log('non anonymous!');
}

// This is similar to the above, but is more
// debugger-friendly, as the name of the function
// will be printed in the debugger.
var nonAnonymous2 = function nonAnonymous2() {
    console.log('non anonymous too!');
};

// This is the syntax for adding event handlers in jQuery
$('field').bind('tap', function(event, data) {
    console.log('binding an anonymous function!');
    event.preventDefault();
});
```

You can also nest functions into functions, creating what is usually called *closures* in Lisp and other functional languages. Closures can access the variables created in the stack of their parent function:

```
function external() {
    var privateVar = 'a private var'; ❶

    function internal() {
        console.log(privateVar); ❷
    }
    return internal; ❸
}

var func = external(); ❹

func(); ❺
```

❶ This variable is "private" in the sense that the code outside of the `external` function cannot access it directly. Remember that variables in JavaScript have function scope, which means that only those functions defined inside of `external` can see it.

❷ The `internal` function prints in the console the contents of the `privateVar` variable.

❸ The `external` function returns the `internal` function.

❹ We assign to the func variable the result of the execution of the external function. This object is a function...

❺ ...that we execute as soon as we can. And the result will be the string "a private var" being shown in the console of the browser.

How to Organize Code in namespaces

When you use lots of libraries in your code, you can easily pick up a function name that corresponds to a pre-existing name in some library that you might have included. To avoid that, you should create namespaces that encapsulate the code of your application:

```
var net = {
    kosmaczewski: {
        adrian: {
            blog: {
                articles: {},
                images: {},
                snippets: {},
                tutorials: {},
                rants: {}
            }
        }
    }
};

// Shortcut (for performance purposes)
var blog = net.kosmaczewski.adrian.blog;
```

Then, you can start adding members (functions, types, variables, etc.) to that namespace:

```
blog.rants.NewRant = function() {
    this.whatever = 'value';
    // code here...
}

blog.images.takePhoto = function() {
    return 'a nice picture';
}

blog.articles.numberOfPosts = 700;
```

Create Objects and Arrays the Easy Way

To create objects and arrays in JavaScript, you can of course use the constructor+methods syntax:

```
var obj = new Object();
var arr = new Array();
```

```
obj.prop = "value";
obj.method = function() {
    console.log('method');
};

arr.push(23);
arr.push("yeah");
arr.push(obj);

arr[2].method();
console.log(arr);
```

While the above syntax is OK, many JavaScript interpreters can handle the following object literal syntax, completely 100% equivalent version, much faster and more Java-Script-like (by this I mean that you are more likely to find this in JavaScript libraries):

```
var obj = {
    prop: "value",
    method: function() {
        console.log('method');
    }
};
var arr = [23, "yeah", obj];

arr[2].method();
console.log(arr);
```

Create a Singleton Object

If you need to create a singleton, yet complex object, do not fall in the classical way of doing things; *do not create a class and then instantiate just one instance!* Since JavaScript objects can be created on the fly, you can use object literals for that.

However, if you need to create just one object, with a complex structure, you can use the following trick:

```
var Singleton = function() {
    var privateValue = "private value";

    return {
        prop: "value",

        method: function() {
            console.log(privateValue);
        }
    };
}();

Singleton.method();  // ❶
```

❶ The trick is in line 11 of the preceding example:

```
}();
```

Do you see the parentheses after the closing bracket and before the semicolon? Well, this triggers the execution of the function, which returns a literal object with methods and properties, and which can reference private members (since they are closures).

This pattern is very common in the Sencha Touch and Ext.js frameworks!

Scheduling Function Execution

Adding a method to the Function class, you can schedule its execution a couple of milliseconds in the future, encapsulating the Window.setTimeout() method:

```
Function.prototype.schedule = function(msec) {
    this.timeout = setTimeout(this, msec);
}

Function.prototype.cancelSchedule = function() {
    clearTimeout(this.timeout);
}

function doSomething() {
    console.log('doSomething');
}

doSomething.schedule(5000);
```

The Sencha Touch framework has a method that does exactly this, called defer().

Concatenating Strings

If you have to concatenate strings, avoid using the + operator whenever possible; an Array instance can be used as a Java StringBuffer or a .NET StringBuilder, as follows:

```
var s = ["a", "long", "array", "of", "strings"];
s.push("is");
s.push("here");
document.write(s.join("<br>"));
```

The above code will display the following output on the web page:

```
a
long
array
of
strings
is
here
```

The use of the join() method is considered as slightly faster than using the + operator, which implies much more object copies in memory, which in turn triggers the garbage collector much more often.

Iterating Over Arrays

When you operate on array objects, you usually end up writing code like this:

```
function operate(obj) {
    console.log(obj);
}

var arr = [54, 25, 68];
for (var i = 0; i < arr.length; ++i) {
    operate(arr[i]);
}
```

But things do not have to be that awful all the time:

```
Array.prototype.each = function(func) {
    for (var i = 0, len = this.length; i < len; i += 1) {
        func(this[i]);
    }
}

function operate(obj) {
    console.log(obj);
}

var arr = [54, 25, 68];
arr.each(operate);
```

Now you have code that is much easier to read, and in particular, it has been tailored for performance!

Using toString() for Reflection

Let's suppose that you have the following code:

```
function Thing() {
    var privateField = "PRIVATE";

    var privateMethod = function() {
        console.log('Private method');
    }

    return {
        publicField: "PUBLIC",

        publicMethod: function() {
            console.log('Public method');
        }
    };
}

// Creating a new instance of "Thing"
var thingy = new Thing();
```

```
// You want to see what's inside, right?
console.log(thingy);
```

The last instruction in the preceding code shows a laconic "[object Object]" that does not tell much about what is inside your object. Actually, the console.log() function, when applied to any JavaScript object, will call the toString() method to its parameter, so try adding a toString() to your objects instead:

```
function Thing() {
    var privateField = "PRIVATE";
    var self = this;

    var privateMethod = function() {
        console.log('Private method');
    }

    return {
        publicField: "PUBLIC",

        publicMethod: function() {
            console.log('Public method');
        },

        toString: function() {
            var re = /function (.*)\(\) {/g;
            var a = self.constructor.toString().split("\n")[0];
            var cls = "Class " + re.exec(a)[1];
            var s = [cls, "", "This is the public API of this class:"];
            for (var item in this) {
                s.push(item);
            }
            return s.join("\n");
        }
    };
}

// Creating a new instance of "Thing"
var thingy = new Thing();

// You'll get a very rudimentary reflection output
console.log(thingy);
```

With this code, you will get this output in a dialog box:

```
Class Thing
```
```
This is the public API of this class:
publicField
publicMethod
```

Easy Code Injection

This code allows you to inject arbitrary code around any function, like if you were doing some AOP-like operations:

```
Function.prototype.wrap = function(before, after) {
    before();
    this();
    after();
};

function doBefore() {
    console.log('do before');
}

function doAfter() {
    console.log('do after');
}

function test() {
    console.log('inside test');
}

// test();
test.wrap(doBefore, doAfter);
```

Object-Oriented Programming in JavaScript

In terms of object orientation, JavaScript has many different syntaxes to provide the same operations. Remember that JavaScript is an object-oriented language without classes; developers can create objects at runtime, and objects have a property called the prototype, which points to the Function object that acts as class of the current object.

Functions are also used to represent classes when doing (object-oriented JavaScript). There are several possible ways to write object-oriented JavaScript code, but they all turn around the concept of the Function class:

```
function Thing() {
    var privateField = "PRIVATE";
    var self = this; ❶

    var privateMethod = function() {
        console.log('Private methods can be called from public methods');
        self.anotherPublicMethod();
    }

    this.publicField = "PUBLIC";

    this.publicMethod = function() {
        privateMethod();
        console.log('From the public method;\nthis is a public value: ' +
this.publicField +
        '\nand this is a private value: ' + privateField);
    };

    this.anotherPublicMethod = function() {
        console.log('You need a trick to call this from a private method!');
    };
```

```
    }

    // Creating a new instance of "Thing"
    var thingy = new Thing();
    thingy.publicMethod();           ❷
```

❶ This is required to be able to use the proper this reference in the privateMethod
   function below. A priori, this points to the currently executing function, which is
   not the behavior that most developers expect. See the following section for a detailed
   discussion about this idiom.

❷ You can also call thingy["publicMethod"]() here; remember that both the array and
   the dot syntaxes are valid and equivalent for accessing object members.

As you can see, methods are just function objects attached as any other property. You
can attach any other function to this property, changing the behavior of your class on
the fly.

The self Trick

As you can see in the previous code, there is a variable called self (it could have any
name) that is equal to this. This is a trick that allows private methods to access public
methods, and you will see it in many JavaScript libraries. The problem can be sum-
marized as follows:

```
    var privateMethod = function() {
        console.log('Private methods can be called from public methods');
        this.anotherPublicMethod();
    }
```

You cannot write the preceding code because this in that context means the private
Method() function. What we want is the this that points to the current Thing() instance.
Yes, it is a bit complex, but it works perfectly well, because the privateMethod() function is a closure and can access the stack variables of the Thing() function. Since self
points to the right object, you can now call the public method that you want.

In summary, this points always to the immediately containing function object where
you are located.

More Ways to Do the Same Thing

Another way to define the Thing class above would be like this, but it has the drawback
that you cannot access the private members, since you are attaching the public members
to the prototype of the function, and as such, you are outside of the main context of
the function, Thing():

```
    function Thing() {
        var privateField = "PRIVATE";

        var privateMethod = function() {
```

```
            console.log('Private methods can be called from public methods');
        }
    }

    Thing.prototype.publicField = "PUBLIC";

    Thing.prototype.publicMethod = function() {
        // privateMethod(); cannot be called here! We are outside of the "Thing()"
        // context
        console.log('From the public method;\nthis is a public value: ' +
            this.publicField + '\nbut you cannot access a private value!');
    };

    // Creating a new instance of "Thing"
    var thingy = new Thing();
    thingy.publicMethod();

    // You can also call the public method as follows:
    thingy["publicMethod"]();
```

The preceding syntax can also be written as follows:

```
    function Thing() {
        var privateField = "PRIVATE";

        var privateMethod = function() {
            console.log('Whatever');
        }
    }

    function Thing_publicMethod() {
        console.log('Implementation');
    };

    function Thing_anotherPublicMethod() {
        console.log('More implementation');
    };

    // "Header file" with the interfaces, all together
    Thing.prototype.publicMethod = Thing_publicMethod;
    Thing.prototype.anotherPublicMethod = Thing_anotherPublicMethod;

    // Creating a new instance of "Thing"
    var thingy = new Thing();
    thingy.publicMethod();
```

which makes all the public methods appear together, like in a good old C or C++
interface header file. Again, some developers might prefer this approach, but you lose
the capability of referencing the private members of your class.

Another Common Way to Create Custom Types

This is another syntax that can be used to create types in JavaScript:

```
function Thing() {
    var privateField = "PRIVATE";

    var privateMethod = function() {
        console.log('Private methods can be called from public methods');
    }

    return {
        publicField: "PUBLIC",

        publicMethod: function() {
            privateMethod();
            console.log('From the public method;\nthis is a public value: ' +
this.publicField +
                '\nand this is a private value: ' + privateField);
        }
    };
}

// Creating a new instance of "Thing"
var thingy = new Thing();
thingy.publicMethod();
```

In this last way of doing things, we are encapsulating the public interface of the class inside the return statement of the class, returning a dictionary (or literal) of members (fields and methods). This creates a neat separation of the public and private parts, with the neat advantage of allowing access to the private fields.

To use this last writing style, remember two things:

- Always remember to separate every member in the return clause with *commas*.
- Always remember to put the return and the *opening curly bracket in the same line!* That is, you *must* write return {, otherwise, since semicolons are optional, the *function will return null!*

 In this book, the syntax above will be preferred and used most often, particularly when dealing with jQuery Mobile applications.

Passing Options

A rather common use case is to pass certain options when instantiating an object. Equally common is it to have a set of default options. If options are passed, they should override the default options. We can allow for this flexibility by writing our function definition like this:

```
function Thing(options) {
    // ...
    var self = this;
```

```
    self.settings = {
      foo: options.foo || "default",
      complex: {
        bar: options.complex.bar || "default bar",
        baz: options.complex.baz || 42
      }
    }

    // ... rest of class

  }
```

Now we can instantiate a new `Thing()` with a hash of options:

```
var default_thing = new Thing();
var custom_thing = new Thing({foo: "Hello World",
                             complex: { baz: 1773 } } )
```

and either the default values are used, or they are overwritten with the ones passed as parameters to the object instantiation.

Conclusion

Great! We have seen in this chapter some useful tricks to keep in mind while you read the code examples in this book, and for your next JavaScript applications. The next chapters will dive into larger frameworks, which all use the idioms and patterns show in the last few pages.

jQuery Mobile

jQuery Mobile[1] is an open source JavaScript UI framework built upon the popular jQuery library, created by John Resig during the last decade.

The development of jQuery Mobile started mid-2010, and quickly became one of the most popular JavaScript frameworks ever. Today jQuery Mobile is used in more mobile web applications than any other framework.

jQuery Mobile is an open source project, hosted on Github (*https://github.com/jquery/ jquery-mobile*) and with a very complete website (*http://jquerymobile.com/*), full of documentation, samples, and references to applications created with the framework.

 At the time of this writing, the current stable version of jQuery Mobile is version 1.1.0. On the other hand, the latest available version of jQuery is 1.7.2.

Supported Platforms

jQuery Mobile works on the vast majority of all modern desktop, smartphone, tablet, and ereader platforms. In addition, feature phones and older browsers are also supported because of a progressive enhancement approach. This is probably one of the most important characteristics of jQuery Mobile.

To provide a quick summary of the browser support in jQuery Mobile, the team has created a simple A (full), B (full minus Ajax), C (basic) grade system with notes of the actual devices and versions where the library has been tested on. The visual fidelity of the experience is highly dependent on CSS rendering capabilities of the device and platform, so not all A grade experience will be pixel-perfect.

---

1. Not to be mistaken with jQTouch, which is a jQuery plug-in, now developed and maintained by Sencha, the same company behind Sencha Touch.

Compatibility

Users of the most advanced mobile browsers can enjoy the full enhanced experience, with Ajax-based animated page transitions; at the time of this writing, this list includes the following operating system/browser combinations:

- iOS since version 3.2
- Android since 2.1
- Windows Phone since version 7
- Blackberry since version 6, including Playbook
- Palm WebOS since 1.4
- Firebox Mobile since 10 beta
- Skyfire since 4.1
- Opera Mobile since 11.5
- Meego since 1.2
- Samsung bada since 2.0
- UC Browser
- Kindle and Kindle Fire
- Nook Color since 1.4.1

An impressive list! All major touchscreen smartphone platforms available today are represented and supported by jQuery Mobile.

On desktop platforms, jQuery Mobile is compatible with Windows, Linux, and Mac OS X versions of the following browsers:

- Safari since version 4
- Chrome since 11
- Firefox since 4
- Internet Explorer since 7
- Opera since 10

One of the greatest benefits from the above lists is that jQuery Mobile is truly one of the most widely compatible mobile frameworks available in the market today. Even better, its large support of desktop browsers allows developers to use many different platforms to build and test their applications. Given that most recent versions of these browsers include developer tools, it also increases its developer appeal.

In Chapter 6 we are going to see in detail how to use the developer consoles of most popular desktop browsers to build mobile applications. For the moment, suffice it to say that you can build your jQuery Mobile applications using any of the desktop browsers mentioned above, and their respective developer tools.

Compatibility with Older Mobile Platforms

But what if our users or requirements specify some older platform? Will jQuery Mobile help us in that case?

jQuery Mobile applications are built on top of standard HTML tags. This means that every jQuery Mobile application is built with graceful degradation by default. Older platforms, not able to display the latest CSS and JavaScript quirks, will quietly default to displaying the HTML structure of these applications, which might or might not be the ideal solution; but there, is, at least, a default answer.

For example, the following browsers have enhanced experience, except without Ajax navigation features:

- Blackberry 5.0
- Opera Mini 5.0 to 6.5
- Nokia Symbian^3

And some other browsers can only enjoy a basic, non-enhanced HTML experience:

- Blackberry 4.x
- Windows Mobile 6 and older
- Older smartphone platforms, including featurephones

Key Features

These are the key features of jQuery Mobile:

- Built on jQuery for familiar and consistent jQuery syntax and minimal learning curve
- Compatible with all major mobile and desktop platforms: iOS, Android, Blackberry, Palm WebOS, Nokia/Symbian, Windows Mobile, Opera Mobile/Mini, Firefox Mobile, and all modern desktop browsers
- Lightweight size (around 20k compressed for all mobile functionality) and minimal image dependencies for speed
- HTML5 Markup-driven configuration of pages and behavior for fast development and minimal required scripting

- Progressive enhancement approach brings core content and functionality to all mobile, tablet, and desktop platforms and a rich, installed application-like experience on newer mobile platforms
- Automatic initialization by using HTML5 data-role attributes in the HTML markup to act as the trigger to automatically initialize all jQuery Mobile widgets found on a page
- Accessibility features such as WAI-ARIA are also included to ensure that the pages work for screen readers (e.g., VoiceOver in iOS) and other assistive technologies
- Touch and mouse event support streamline the process of supporting touch, mouse, and cursor focus-based user input methods with a simple API
- UI widgets enhance native controls with touch-optimized, themable controls
- Powerful theming framework and ThemeRoller application make highly branded experiences easy to build

At a Glance

The most important thing to know about jQuery Mobile is that *it is a UI library, not a jQuery plug-in*. It is a library that will take valid HTML tags as input, and will format them using predefined styles and adapting them to the current browser capabilities. It is not a complete framework like .NET, Java, or even Sencha Touch, which provide lower-level services like serialization, storage, or networking. jQuery Mobile relies upon JavaScript and the HTML5 features supported by the hosting browser to offer extended functionality.

This first characteristic determines the tremendous mobile browser support of jQuery Mobile, while at the same time explaining why developers have to roll their own Java-Script code to implement complex behaviors, to implement storage, or to interact with the hardware features exposed by the host browser (geolocation, compass, etc.).

Another important characteristic of jQuery Mobile is that it does not impose any kind of structure to the JavaScript code of your system; the main component of the application being the HTML files that define the semantic of the user interface, but not its ultimate look and feel. In general, developers will apply behavior using standard jQuery syntaxes and idioms, just as with any regular web page.

To Do List Application

To demonstrate how to create applications with jQuery Mobile, we are going to build a very simple application with it: a to do list application, shown in Figure 3-1. The application will have the following set of features:

- The application has two screens: a task list and a task form.
- Upon launch, the task list is shown.

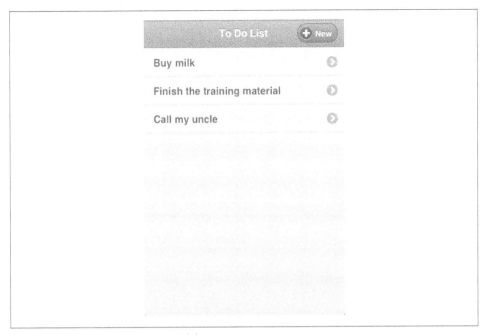

Figure 3-1. To Do App in jQuery Mobile

- The user can select a task from the list, or create a new one with a specific button on the interface.
- The task form allows the user to modify the parameter of a single task.
- When editing an existing task, the user can remove it from the list just by tapping on a "Delete task" button at the bottom of the screen.

Given that jQuery Mobile is just a UI framework, and as such does not provide a built-in persistence mechanism, we are going to use one of the most hyped new features of HTML5: the local storage.

The HTML File

The core section of the application is, undoubtedly, the HTML file. jQuery Mobile is not a JavaScript-intensive framework, but rather one that relies upon special HTML tags and attributes to get the work done. However, we are going to use JavaScript later, to add behavior to the whole thing.

First things first: this is the basic HTML5 file we need. Let's name it *index.html*:

```
<!DOCTYPE html>
<html>
    <head>
        <meta charset="utf-8">
        <meta name="apple-mobile-web-app-capable" content="yes">
```

```
        <meta name="viewport" content="initial-scale = 1.0, user-scalable = no">
        <title>To Do List</title>
        <link rel="stylesheet" href="../../_libs/jqm/jquery.mobile-1.1.0.min.css">
        <script src="../../_libs/jqm/jquery-1.7.2.min.js"></script>
        <script src="../../_libs/jqm/jquery.mobile-1.1.0.min.js"></script>
        <script src="app.js"></script> ❶
    </head>
    <body>
    </body>
</html>
```

❶ We are also going to create a file named *app.js*, which will contain the JavaScript code that will bring the behavior to our application. Let's just create the file alongside our *index.html* file.

As you can see, we require a very basic `<head>` structure, with just the following files included:

- The latest jQuery library
- The latest jQuery Mobile JavaScript file
- The latest jQuery Mobile CSS file
- Our own *app.js* file

Pages

A jQuery Mobile application consists of *pages*. Following Apple's own definition of screens in the world of iOS, each page represents a screenful of data. What is a page? In jQuery Mobile parlance, a page is a simple `<div>` element with the `data-role="page"` tags:

```
<div data-role="page" id="indexPage">
</div>
```

You can have as many `data-role="page"` element in your HTML file. However, many developers choose to separate their pages in different HTML files, and have jQuery Mobile manage the navigation among these files. We are going to use this approach, which is recommended, for having a more organized application. But keep in mind that nothing prevents you from using a single HTML file instead.

Accessing Pages from JavaScript

Just like any other HTML element, you can access jQuery Mobile page elements using the typical jQuery syntax: `var indexPage = $('#indexPage')` would return a pointer to the HTML `<div>` defined in the previous snippet. As you might imagine, it is then fundamental to have different IDs for every element.

This is great news for web developers, who are able to reuse their current knowledge of web applications in the realm of mobile web apps.

A jQuery Mobile `page` is usually composed of three basic elements: a `header`, a content, and a `footer`, as you might have guessed:

```
<div data-role="page" id="indexPage">
    <div data-role="header">
        Header
    </div>

    <div data-role="content">
        Content
    </div>

    <div data-role="footer">
        Footer
    </div>
</div>
```

Let's stop for a minute, and see what we have here in Figure 3-2.

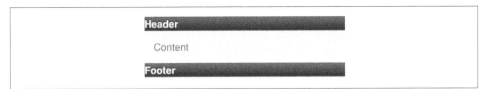

Figure 3-2. First Screen with jQuery Mobile

As you can see, our first page already features a basic structure, but visually it is not very appealing. Furthermore, neither the header nor the footer stay in place when you scroll the application with your finger. Let's make things nicer with a couple of attributes:

```
<div data-role="page" id="indexPage" data-theme="b">
    <div data-role="header" data-position="fixed" data-theme="b">
        <h1>Header</h1>
    </div>

    <div data-role="content">
        Content
    </div>

    <div data-role="footer" data-position="fixed" data-theme="b">
        <h1>Footer</h1>
    </div>
</div>
```

And let's see how this looks in Figure 3-3.

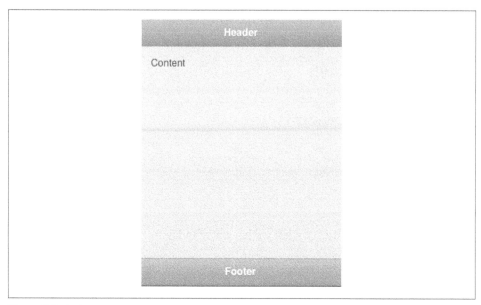

Figure 3-3. A nicer screen

Much nicer indeed! Even better, the header and the footer stay in place when the user scrolls the application; exactly the behavior we want in our application. The data-role, data-theme, and data-position tags provide metadata information that is used by jQuery Mobile to render the page properly.

What is with those data- attributes?

jQuery Mobile uses data- attributes to apply styles, semantics, and even behavior to standard HTML elements. HTML5 is flexible enough so that it can be extended with nonstandard attributes, as long as they start with the data- prefix. Given that browsers usually ignore unknown tags and attributes, it is safe to assume that these extensions downgrade gracefully.

Thanks to this trick, jQuery Mobile is able to display enhanced content in the latest browsers, while displaying standard web content in older browsers, not supporting the latest JavaScript and CSS features.

Lists

Lists are a pervasive widgets in most UI toolkits. They are fundamental to show sequential data, to layout screen widgets in order, and to provide choices and perspective to the user. We have said previously that jQuery Mobile uses standard HTML tags, which are styled and presented as touchscreen controls when rendered in the modern browsers.

Lists are no exception to this rule, and jQuery Mobile uses standard `<ul>` tags, with their typical child `<li>` elements, to represent lists. Of course, the `<ul>` element will be "augmented" with `data-role="listview"` tag providing the required metadata, so that jQuery Mobile displays them as users expect them in touchscreen smartphones.

This is how you create a list in jQuery Mobile:

```
<div data-role="content">
    <ul data-role="listview">
      <li>First element</li>
      <li>Second element</li>
      <li>Third element</li>
    </ul>
</div>
```

And Figure 3-4 shows how the list appears when rendered.

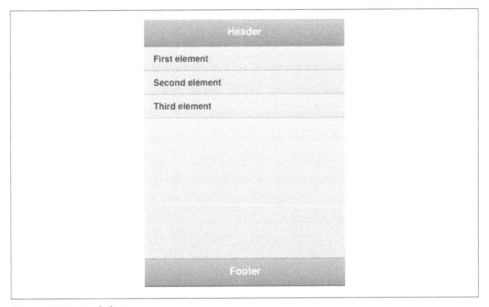

Figure 3-4. A simple list

As you can imagine, we are going to use this list to represents the different to-do items entered by our user. For that, it is very important for the user to be able to touch an individual item in the list to edit it, and ideally to be able to mark tasks as done in this very screen as well.

For that, we are going to add simple `<a>` tags inside of our `<li>` elements, and jQuery Mobile will transform them automatically into touchable elements:

```
<div data-role="content">
    <ul data-role="listview" data-theme="c">
      <li><a href="#first">First element</a></li>
      <li><a href="#second">Second element</a></li>
```

```
    <li><a href="#third">Third element</a></li>
    </ul>
</div>
```

Finally, we are also going to add a button at the right-most end of each row, which will be used by the user to set any task as done. This is very easy to achieve, just by adding a secondary `<a>` element inside the `<li>`:

```
<div data-role="content">
    <ul data-role="listview" data-theme="c">
        <li><a href="#first">First element</a>
            <a href="#setasdone"></a></li>
        <li><a href="#second">Second element</a>
            <a href="#setasdone"></a></li>
        <li><a href="#third">Third element</a>
            <a href="#setasdone"></a></li>
    </ul>
</div>
```

Figure 3-5 shows how our customized list looks so far.

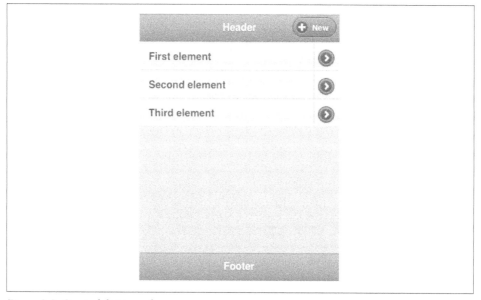

Figure 3-5. Our task list is ready

Buttons

We need now a means to create a new task on our application. For that, we are going to add a button on the user interface. When the user clicks the button, a new instance of a task will be created, and shown on the task form.

Creating buttons on jQuery Mobile is very easy: just use an `<a>` element with a `data-role="button"` in it, and you are done:

```
<div data-role="header" data-position="fixed" data-theme="b">
    <h1>Header</h1>
    <a href="#formPage" data-role="button">New</a>
</div>
```

If you run the preceding code, you will see the button appear on the left side of the screen. Should you want it on the right side, you should add `class="ui-btn-right"` to the item.

Finally, if you would like an icon on your button, you could add the `data-icon="plus"` attribute, and your button would appear as shown in Figure 3-6.

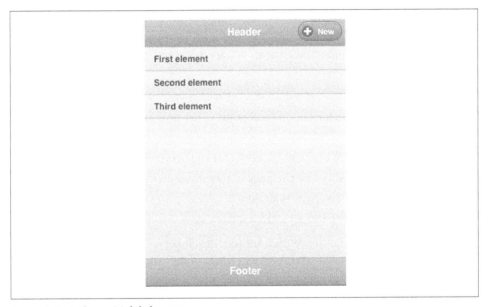

Figure 3-6. A jQuery Mobile button

Customizing the Look and Feel

We have seen so far quite a few ways to change the look and feel of our application:

- You can use the `data-theme` attribute; this has the effect of applying a default style, provided by jQuery Mobile, or one that you have defined on your own. We are going to see at the end of this chapter how to define our own style to the application we are building.

- You can also add specific `class` attributes to your UI elements; given that jQuery Mobile applications are defined using standard HTML and CSS, you can use all the usual arsenal to provide a beautiful style to your application.

Navigation

As described in our feature list above, our To Do List application has two screens; the first is the list of the to-do items, and the second is the form used to create and update items.

To navigate from one screen to another, the answer is just to use pure HTML! As you can see in the snippet above, the New button in the toolbar is just an `<a>` tag with an `href="#formPage"` tag, styled using special `data-icon` and `class` tags, which provide the look and feel that we want for our application.

Page Lifecycle

So far the only thing we have done is write HTML code. Where is the JavaScript? Well, as Maximiliano Firtman would say, jQuery Mobile is not a JavaScript coder paradise; a priori you can describe the look and feel and most of the navigation behaviour just by writing HTML pages and linking them. We are, however, going to see how to script jQuery Mobile applications.

And the first thing that we are going to do, is to hook ourselves to some events.

In a similar fashion to Sencha Touch (and many other mobile UI toolkits such as iOS and Android), jQuery Mobile pages also have lifecycle events:

- `pageinit`: called before the page is shown for the first time
- `pagebeforeshow`: called before the page is actually shown
- `pageshow`: called after the page is shown
- `pagehide`: called after the page is hidden from view

These events will be familiar to iOS and Android developers, as they closely reassemble those of the UIViewController and Activity classes in iOS and Android, respectively.

As you can imagine, you can attach functions to these events, and they will be executed when the time comes. Let's take a look at how we use these events in our application:

```
$("#formPage").live("pagebeforeshow", function(event) {
    if (ToDoList.currentTask === null) {
        $("#formPageTitle").text("New Task");
        $("#taskName").val("");
        $("#deleteButton").hide();
    }
    else {
        ToDoList.taskManager.getTaskById(ToDoList.currentTask, function(task) {
            ToDoList.currentTask = task;
            $("#formPageTitle").text("Update Task");
            $("#taskName").val(ToDoList.currentTask.name());
            $("#deleteButton").show();
        });
    }
});
```

In the preceding code, we check whether we are showing a new task, or one that exists in the local storage already. We set the user interface properly before showing the page, so that the user will be presented with a usable form later.

Forms

jQuery Mobile uses the most simple HTML when dealing with forms. Instead of creating the widgets with JavaScript code, a simple <form> will be used:

```
<form action="" method="post" id="form">
    <ul data-role="listview" id="taskDetailsFields">
        <li data-role="list-divider">Task details:</li>
        <li data-role="fieldcontain">
            <label for="taskName">Name:</label>
            <input type="text" name="taskName" id="taskName" value="" />
        </li>

        <li data-role="fieldcontain">
            <label for="taskDescription">Description:</label>
            <textarea cols="40" rows="8" name="taskDescription"
                id="taskDescription"></textarea>
        </li>

        <li data-role="fieldcontain">
            <label for="taskCompleted">Completed:</label>
            <select name="taskCompleted" id="taskCompleted" data-role="slider">
                <option value="no">No</option>
                <option value="yes">Yes</option>
            </select>
        </li>

    <!-- ...snip... -->
```

As you can see, these are exactly the same controls that would be used in a standard web form; jQuery Mobile will adapt these visual elements to the screen of the current device.

> The principle of graceful degradation applies here; older devices will display a fully working form, without any special styles, and the functionality of the application will (should, at least) remain the same.

When touching the "Save" button, the form fields are read using standard jQuery notation:

```
var task = {
    name: $("#taskName").val(),
    description: $("#taskDescription").val(),
    completed: ($("#taskCompleted").val() === "yes"),
    duedate: $("#taskDuedate").data("datebox").theDate
};
```

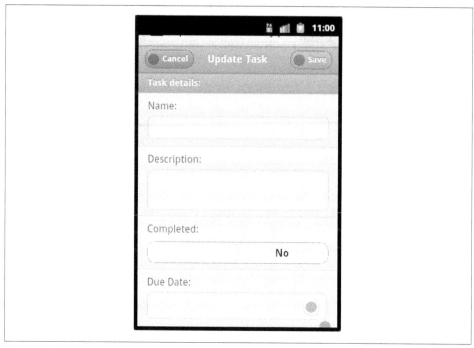

Figure 3-7. Task Editor of the jQuery Mobile App

Plug-ins

jQuery Mobile has an open architecture, allowing developers to extend and provide new functionality to the framework as required, all while keeping a lean and understandable core system. We are going to use a particular plug-in to provide users with a useful user interface widget, not included natively with jQuery Mobile: a date picker.

The To Do List application allows individual tasks to have a target date defined; however, jQuery Mobile, unlike Sencha Touch, does not provide a native control to select dates in a visual manner. To solve this problem, we are going to use an extension to jQuery Mobile: the jQuery Mobile Datebox (*https://github.com/jtsage/jquery-mobile -datebox*), A multi-mode date and time picker for jQueryMobile.

This is how you define an input field with the `data-role="datebox"` tag, so that the date picker can provide a proper UI to the user:

```
<li data-role="fieldcontain">
    <label for="taskDuedate">Due Date:</label>
    <input name="taskDuedate" id="taskDuedate" type="date" data-role="datebox"
    data-options='{"mode": "calbox", "disableManualInput": true}'>
</li>
```

Figure 3-8. jQuery Mobile Datebox

There is a long list of available plug-ins in the jQuery Mobile resources page (*http:// jquerymobile.com/resources/#Plugins*).

Storage

Well! After all the HTML we have written, we would think that the application is ready; however, if you refresh your browser, you are going to see that all the tasks that you have defined are not persisted, and you have to enter them again. Not at all the desired behavior. However, given that jQuery Mobile does not provide a standard way to save information in a local HTML5 database, we are using the standard HTML5 local storage instead.

First, we are going to encapsulate the storage logic in a `MyTaskListApp` object, which will be used throughout the application. This object will be a singleton object, built using the Singleton paradigm described previously, which employs an anonymous function, called only once during the life of the application:

```
var MyTaskListApp = function () {}();
```

This function will return what I call a public interface, which is basically a literal object bundled with functions. These functions will reference internal, private variables, which will hold the internal state of the application, isolated from the rest of the system:

```
var MyTaskListApp = function () {
    return {};
}();
```

Pay attention to the way this code is written; to avoid mayhem in the sequence of brackets (round, curly, and square), it is recommended to always write them in order, opening and closing them at the same time. This simple technique helps developers to avoid mistakes and to advance faster in their programming tasks.

This singleton object will provide several methods that will allow us to manipulate the state of our application; let us just stub them at the moment, and we will deal with the internals later:

```
var MyTaskListApp = function () {
    return {
        init: function () {},
        displayCurrentTask: function() {},
        saveCurrentTask: function() {},
        refreshTasks: function() {},
        addTask: function () {},
        removeCurrentTask: function() {},
        setCurrentTask: function() {}
    };
}();
```

Of course, we are going to define a Task model class, that we are going to expose to the rest of the application; for this, we are going to use a very simple, rather classic Java-Script function that can be used with the new operator, as usual:

```
MyTaskListApp.Task = function () {
    this.done = false;
    this.title = "New Task";
    this.description = "Empty task";
    this.dueDate = new Date();
};
```

Our controller object will hold an array of instances of this Task class. Let's begin by implementing the addTask function:

```
var MyTaskListApp = function () {

    var tasks = [];

    return {
        // ...

        addTask: function (task) {
            tasks.push(task);
        },

        // ...
    };
}();
```

As can be seen, the implementation is as simple as it gets; however, if we want to use the HTML5 local storage we need to somehow synchronize the in-memory storage provided by the tasks array, and the browser's own localStorage. Let's do that now:

```
var MyTaskListApp = function () {

    var tasks = [];
    var TASKS_KEY = 'jQueryTasks';

    var loadTasks = function () {
```

```
        if (localStorage) {
            var storedTasks = localStorage[TASKS_KEY];
            if (!storedTasks) {
                // This could mean that the application is running for the first
                // time, or that the developer has deleted the object from the
                // local storage
                saveTasks();
            }
            else {
                tasks = JSON.parse(storedTasks);
            }
        }
    };

    var saveTasks = function () {
        if (localStorage) {
            localStorage[TASKS_KEY] = JSON.stringify(tasks);
        }
    };

    return {
        init: function () {
            loadTasks();
        },
        // ...

        addTask: function (task) {
            tasks.push(task);
            saveTasks();
        },

        // ...
    };
}();
```

In the preceding code we have introduced two private functions in our controller; they are used to wrap the access to the `localStorage` from the rest of the application, which might help us in the future should we choose to change the storage strategy later. The methods in the public interface of the controller will use this methods repeatedly, to guarantee the synchronization between the array and the `localStorage`.

Codiqa

One of the most imaginative uses of jQuery Mobile is without any doubt Codiqa (*http://codiqa.com/*) (see Figure 3-9), a browser-based UI prototyping application that can be used to create mockups of mobile applications. It is entirely based on jQuery Mobile, and even the main site of jQuery Mobile (*http://jquerymobile.com/*) features Codiqa.

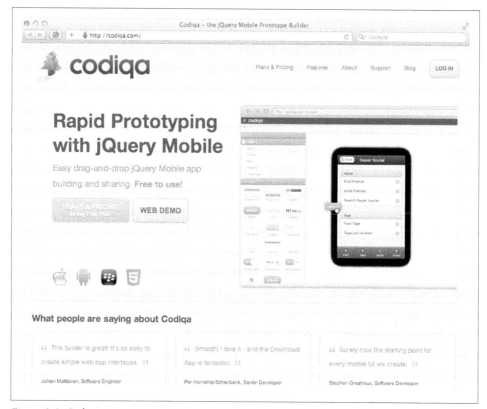

Figure 3-9. Codiqa

ThemeRoller

The ThemeRoller for jQuery Mobile (*http://jquerymobile.com/themeroller/index.php*) is a web application created by the jQuery Mobile team, that allows developers to create the stylesheet for their applications with a very convenient visual interface.

Figure 3-10 shows the interface of the ThemeRoller for jQuery Mobile, which provides a download link for the resulting CSS file, in both minified and non-minified formats, including all the sprite images used by the stylesheets.

The snippet below shows a fragment of the non-minified CSS generated by the ThemeRoller, which includes all kinds of comments to guide developers into customizing the final style:

```
/*
* jQuery Mobile Framework 1.0.1
* http://jquerymobile.com
*
* Copyright 2011-2012 (c) jQuery Project
* Dual licensed under the MIT or GPL Version 2 licenses.
* http://jquery.org/license
```

```
 *
 */
/* Swatches */

/* A
---------------------------------------------*/

.ui-bar-a .ui-link-inherit {
    color: #ffffff /*{a-bar-color}*/;
}
.ui-bar-a .ui-link {
    color:  #7cc4e7  /*{a-bar-link-color}*/;
    font-weight: bold;
}

.ui-bar-a .ui-link:hover {
    color:  #2489CE  /*{a-bar-link-hover}*/;
}
```

Figure 3-10. ThemeRoller for jQuery Mobile

Conclusion

jQuery Mobile provides a simpler way to build mobile apps, with broader browser support than Sencha Touch, but with a smaller set of prebuilt functionalities and widgets. It requires only a simple toolset, with lots of simplicity, and the learning curve is as easy as it could be.

In my personal experience, jQuery Mobile is perfect for the following scenarios:

Strong cross-browser application framework
In this area, jQuery Mobile is simple unbeatable and offers incredible flexibility in a very large range of mobile platforms.

Quick prototyping tool for mobile applications
Designers can quickly test ideas with their customers, modeling interactions, and navigations without any code at all just by using HTML standards. The product of the design process can even be reused by developers for the creation of the final version of the application.

CHAPTER 4

Sencha Touch

Of all the frameworks presented in this book, Sencha Touch is probably the most complex and daunting of all. It is an amazing piece of JavaScript code, providing application developers with a fertile playground ready to be explored.

This chapter will provide an introduction to Sencha Touch, and will later explore its characteristics by creating three small applications from scratch.

 At the time of this writing, the current stable version of Sencha Touch is version 2.0.1.

Introduction and History

Sencha Touch is a fully fledged UI framework, in the same tradition as Cocoa Touch, Swing, or .NET. It is completely written in JavaScript, and it is a direct spin-off of the famous Ext.js framework, initially created in 2006 by Jack Slocum as an extension (hence the name) of the YUI framework from Yahoo!.

Sencha Touch provides a set of very complex widgets, reacting to the most complex gestures, geared towards the creation of extremely complex web applications. In this sense, Sencha Touch (and Ext.js) can be compared to Cappuccino (*http://cappuccino .org/*), SproutCore (*http://sproutcore.com/*), or other large-scale, enterprise-y frameworks.

Characteristics

And enterprise-y it is. Or at least that is how Sencha (the company behind Sencha Touch) is aggressively marketing it. Frameworks falling into this category usually have the following characteristics:

* (Relatively) Large code footprint

- Complex object hierarchy
- Long list of widgets, with complex customizations, ready to be used out-of-the-box
- Opinionated approaches to common tasks
- Cross-browser support
- Detailed documentation and a fanatical user base
- Commercial support

Sencha Touch largely fills all of the requirements above, including the availability of an advanced designer tool: the Sencha Architect 2. This tool can be used to visually design user interfaces, using a tool similar to Interface Builder or Visual Studio, allowing developers to quickly create prototypes or complex user interfaces without having to write a single line of code. We are going to learn abut Sencha Architect at the end of this chapter.

Supported Platforms

Sencha Touch is a product of Sencha, which was formed after popular JavaScript library projects Ext.JS, jQTouch and Raphaël were combined. The first release of Sencha Touch was version 0.90 beta on July 17, 2010. This beta release supported iOS devices like iPhone, iPod touch, the iPad, and Android devices.

Subsequently, the first stable version 1.0 was released in November 2010. The latest stable version 2.0.1 adds support to BlackBerry devices running OS version 6. Version 2.0 has been released as Beta during SenchaCon 2011, held in Austin, Texas in October 2011, and in final version during the writing of this book, in March 2012.

Webkit Only!

It is very important to note that *Sencha Touch is primarily based on Webkit, so it can support only webkit-based browsers like Chrome and Safari*. This fact has a direct implication in the development process, because it means that you cannot use Firefox or Firebug to debug the application, and instead you have to use the equivalent tools provided by Safari or Chrome.

Key Features

Sencha Touch has several features that set it apart from other similar frameworks; in this section we are going to see some of them in detail.

GUI Controls

Sencha Touch includes a set of GUI-based controls or components for use within mobile web applications. These components are highly optimized for touch input.

Some GUI components available in the library:

- Buttons with device specific themes and effects
- Form elements like text fields (for email, date picker, address, etc.), sliders, selectors, and comboboxes
- List component, which has momentum scrolling along with index
- Minimalistic icon set
- Toolbars/Menus
- Movable tabs
- Bottom toolbars
- Map component with support to multi-touch input like pinch and zoom
- All the components can be themed according to the target device (this is done using SASS, a stylesheet language built over CSS)

To demonstrate the large choice of GUI components available in Sencha Touch, the development team has built the Kitchen Sink (*http://dev.sencha.com/deploy/touch/examples/kitchensink/*), a rather extensive demo showcasing almost every possible control available in the library; you can take a look at the Figure 4-1.

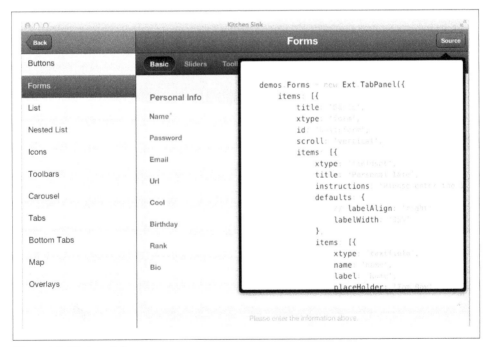

Figure 4-1. Kitchen sink

CSS Transitions and Animations

Sencha Touch has certain built-in transition effects, based on the powerful CSS3 support that newer Webkit browsers have:

• Slide over or under current element
• Pop
• Flips
• Cube

Touch Event Management

Sencha Touch supports common touch gestures basically built from Touch events that are web standard but are supported only by iOS, Android OS, and some touch-enabled devices:

• Tap
• Double Tap
• Swipe
• Scroll
• Pinch

However, care must be taken when handling many events in the same panel; for example, when handling single and double taps, the single tap event should trigger the creation of a delayed task, that should be removed if the user taps twice. It is somewhat unfortunate that the framework does not handle this situation by itself.

Application Data Support

Sencha Touch consists of both UI libraries and also data libraries. With the use of data libraries the mobile web application can get data from any remote server. Sencha Touch has a data package to support web standards for data interchange with server like AJAX and JSONP. It also supports YQL. Using these technologies, data can be bound to visual components like lists to reflect data from server.

One of the most interesting aspects of Sencha Touch regarding data management is the fact that lists (and other DataView panels) can be bound to data stores in such a way that they will be notified automatically of any change in the data store. Developers do not have to manually reload the list to reflect the changes in the data!

JavaScript Idioms

Sencha Touch has inherited from Ext.js a standardized (and opinionated) way of writing JavaScript; this has the advantage of simplifying the reading of code using these frameworks, but it also sometimes represents a slightly steep curve for developers new to the platform.

We are then going to spend a bit of time learning the classic Ext.js JavaScript idiom, which will make things easier to understand later on. Developers who have prior experience with Ext.js can jump or skim this section altogether, and start writing their first Sencha Touch application right away.

The idioms used by Sencha Touch are two:

- Dictionaries for widgets
- Method-based definition of classes and creation of instances

This section will describe these two patterns in detail.

Descriptive Dictionary Pattern

The first, most common idiom used by Sencha Touch is what I call the Descriptive Dictionary Pattern. Whenever you create a new instance of any Sencha Touch class, you are going to pass a dictionary of options to the function. For example, when you create your application, you write code like the following:

```
Ext.application({});
```

The `Ext.application` function takes a single parameter, a dictionary with options that are used to modify the behavior and look and feel of the application. Among those parameters, there are two very important ones that we are going to add:

name
> A simple string without spaces used to generate a master namespace where all the objects of our application will be stored. This is similar to creating a global `application` JavaScript object, but instead Sencha Touch takes care of its creation automatically for us.

launch
> This parameter takes a function and for all practical purposes, it is the entry point of the execution of our application.

Having said that, let me introduce to you a reasonable "Hello world" application in Sencha Touch 2:

```
Ext.application({
    name: 'SampleApp',
    launch: function() {
        Ext.Msg.alert('Hello, World!');
    }
});
```

Our objective is of course to create complex user interfaces; for that, we are going to use the singleton `Ext.Viewport` object, which serves a similar purpose as the default

UIWindow instance used in iOS applications. The basic canvas where any other widgets can be drawn.

Just call the add() function of the singleton Ext.Viewport object to add any required subviews:

```
Ext.application({
    name: 'SampleApp',
    launch: function() {
        Ext.Viewport.add({});
    }
});
```

Just like when calling the Ext.application() method, the Ext.Viewport.add() function also takes a literal object as parameter; you just specify a dictionary with the proper types, and let Sencha Touch do the rest:

```
Ext.application({
    name: 'SampleApp',
    launch: function() {
        Ext.Viewport.add({      ❶
            xtype: 'tabpanel'
        });
    }
});
```

❶ The object defined in this dictionary has the xtype property, which is very common in Sencha Touch.

We are going to learn more about the xtype property later in this chapter; for the moment, suffice to say that this parameter is used to determine the class of the object that will be created by Sencha Touch inside our Viewport object.

Object Orientation in Sencha Touch

Sencha Touch provides an abstraction around JavaScript's own object orientation system, allowing developers to manage, in a small set of functions, the definition of classes and the creation of instances from those classes. In short, you use the Ext.define() function to... well, define a new class, and you use the Ext.create() function to create a new instance from any class.

For example, let's see how to define a new Sencha Touch class:

```
Ext.define('ToDoListApp.model.Task', {
    extend: 'Ext.data.Model',

    config: {
        fields: [{
            name: 'id',
            type: 'int'
        },

        {
```

```
            name: 'completed',
            type: 'boolean'
        },

        {
            name: 'dueDate',
            type: 'date'
        },

        {
            name: 'title',
            type: 'string'
        },

        {
            name: 'description',
            type: 'string'
        }
        ],
        idProperty: 'id'
    }

    constructor: function(title) {
        if (title) {
            this.title = title;
        }

        return this;
    },

    markAsCompleted: function() {
        console.log(this.title + " is done!");
        this.completed = true;
    }
});
```

Now let's see how we create a new instance from the class we have previously defined:

```
var task = Ext.create('ToDoListApp.model.Task', { title: 'Buy milk' });
task.markAsCompleted(); // logs "Buy milk: is done!" in the console
```

In the preceding code, we are not using the new keyword provided by JavaScript: new ToDoListApp.model.Task(). Instead, it is recommended to use Ext.create, since it allows you to take advantage of dynamic loading, which is a core feature of Sencha Touch.

Learn About the Sencha Touch Class System

It is strongly recommended to read the Class System Guide (*http://docs .sencha.com/ext-js/4-0/#!/guide/class_system*) to learn more about the idioms used by Ext.js and Sencha Touch for defining and using classes.

Creating a To Do List App

The first application we are going to create with Sencha Touch is a very simple To Do List that allows users to:

- Browse a list of tasks
- Mark a task as completed (or not) by double tapping the task
- Tasks are grouped by due date, so that it is easier to see what has to be done in each day
- Add, edit, and remove tasks from the list

Finally, we are going to build this application as a single JavaScript file to begin with. We are going to break it into a proper MVC application after we have a working app. (See Figure 4-2.)

Figure 4-2. Sencha Touch To Do List

Create the HTML

The first thing to do is to create the HTML file that will hold the different pieces of the application. In our case, it will look like this:

```
<!DOCTYPE html>
<html>
  <head>
```

```
      <meta charset="utf-8" />
      <title>Hello World</title>

      <script src="sencha/sencha-touch.js"></script>
      <link href="sencha/resources/css/sencha-touch.css" rel="stylesheet" />

      <script src="app.js"></script>
    </head>
    <body></body>
  </html>
```

At this point you might ask yourself, but wasn't Sencha supposed to be a JavaScript-only framework? Well, yes, but we need at least one HTML file for the browser to load all the different pieces of our application.

The HTML code itself is extremely simple; it just loads the two main files of the Sencha Touch framework: the JavaScript and the CSS stylesheet. The <body> tag, in particular, is completely empty, as Sencha Touch takes care of the complete initialization of any application built with it.

The biggest downside of Sencha Touch can be easily seen right now: the huge size of the library means that, in slow hardware, loading a Sencha Touch application can take up to a couple of seconds, which might or might not be acceptable for your users. Of course, as per Moore's law, as mobile devices grow more powerful, this is becoming less and less of a problem (however, as this happens, these libraries keep growing, so it is a continuous fight between ease of development and performance, as a matter of fact).

Starting the Application Code

The code of the application is located in the *app.js* file. Remember that Sencha Touch is a pure JavaScript framework, and as such you create, manipulate, and destroy HTML elements through JavaScript, without ever writing a single line of HTML.

The first thing we are going to do is to create the basic skeleton of our application. This skeleton is constituted by the following elements:

- An instance of Ext.Application, which is the base class for Sencha Touch applications. When a Sencha Touch application starts, the entry point is always the launch() method of this instance.
- A master viewport panel, created by the application instance, which plays the same role as the UIWindow in an iPhone app, or the default activity in an Android application.
- Inside the viewport, we are going to embed all the other screens, each stored in a separate variable (later, we will see how to embed these elements in separate files to create a more manageable application structure).

Let's see the code that represents what we have just described:

```
Ext.Loader.setConfig({
    enabled: true
});

Ext.application({
    models: [
        'Task'
    ],

    controllers: [
        'TaskController'
    ],

    stores: [
        'TaskStore'
    ],

    views: [
        'TaskList',
        'TaskForm'
    ],

    name: 'ToDoListApp',

    launch: function() {
        Ext.Viewport.add([
                        Ext.create('ToDoListApp.view.TaskList'),
                        Ext.create('ToDoListApp.view.TaskForm')
        ]);
    }
});
```

If you remember our discussion about JavaScript at the beginning of this book, you will remember that it is important to scope the variables of a JavaScript application, so that the global namespace is not cluttered. This is what we are doing here: the ToDo-ListApp name is automatically converted by Sencha Touch in a variable, which works both as a pointer to the application instance and as a namespace in itself, where all the different widgets of the application will reside.

We can also see that the launch() method calls the Ext.Viewport.add() method of the Viewport singleton, which holds two instances of custom panels. You can think of a Container as an UIView in iOS or a View in Android; Containers are the basic building visual block of Sencha Touch applications.

And, similarly to other UI frameworks, you can embed Containers into Containers; the particularity in Sencha Touch is the use of the items property, which takes an array of Containers. This property simply adds the containers as children of the current one, and if you pass more than one container, the first is shown while the others are hidden.

Another important element of the definition above is the fact that Sencha Touch Viewports automatically use the layout: "card" instruction. This tells the container to use an instance of Ext.layout.CardLayout to display its children items, and it makes the parent only display a child container at a time. The `CardLayout` class also provides a `setActiveItem()` method that we are going to use in this application, in order to jump from container to container, using animations.

Transitions

One interesting property of the items property is that you can add several children panels to a parent panel, and then you can navigate from screen to screen, using similar animations as if you were using an UINavigationController in iOS. However, there is a greater flexibility to specify the types of animations, all powered using WebKit's own CSS animations.

Creating Instances

Sencha Touch elements can be created both by using the `Ext.create` function, which requires the class name of the object, or by using dictionaries with the xtype keyword, which takes a special code as a parameter. When reading this parameter, Sencha Touch will automatically create the object of the corresponding class.

The following table shows the correspondence of the different classes available in Sencha Touch.

Table 4-1. Equivalence between instance creation syntaxes

Category	xtype	Class
Basic	button	Ext.Button
	component	Ext.Component
	container	Ext.Container
	dataview	Ext.DataView
	panel	Ext.Panel
	toolbar	Ext.Toolbar
	spacer	Ext.Spacer
	tabpanel	Ext.TabPanel
Form	form	Ext.form.FormPanel
	checkbox	Ext.form.Checkbox
	select	Ext.form.Select
	field	Ext.form.Field
	fieldset	Ext.form.FieldSet
	hidden	Ext.form.Hidden
	numberfield	Ext.form.NumberField
	radio	Ext.form.Radio

Category	xtype	Class
	slider	Ext.form.Slider
	textarea	Ext.form.TextArea
	textfield	Ext.form.TextField
Data	store	Ext.data.Store
	arraystore	Ext.data.ArrayStore
	jsonstore	Ext.data.JsonStore
	xmlstore	Ext.data.XmlStore

To use the xtype syntax, just create a standard JavaScript dictionary and use it in the items or dockeditems property of your panel, just as if you would use any other instance:

```
Ext.define('ToDoListApp.view.TaskList', {
    extend: 'Ext.dataview.List',

    config: {

        items: [{
            xtype: 'toolbar',
            title: 'To Do List',
            items: [{
                xtype: 'spacer'
            },
            {
                xtype: 'button',
                iconCls: 'add',
                ui: 'plain'
            }]
        }]
    }
});
```

Stores, Proxies, Writers, and Readers

The diagram in Figure 4-3 shows the typical organization of a Sencha Touch 2 application. In this organization, the MVC standard is complemented by a series of supplementary objects, which serve as an abstraction layer for the underlying storage and communication mechanisms used by the application.

The first element in this mechanism is the *Store*. A Store represents an abstraction around data.

Views use stores directly (hence the direct connection between views and stores in Figure 4-3). One of the coolest features of this direct relationship is that views are 100% aware and dependent on the state of a store; this means that if you want to update a UI element attached to a store, you just update the store data, and the UI element will

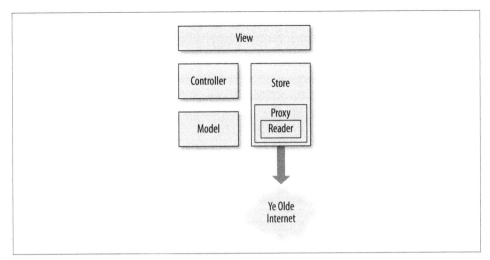

Figure 4-3. Sencha Touch 2 application architecture

be updated automatically. This is a common mechanism in ASP.NET, for example, where it is known as data binding.

There are several different kinds of stores available:

- `Ext.data.Store` is the base class used to represent stores; usually applications just create a raw instance of this class and use it as a store.
- `Ext.data.TreeStore` is used to represent hierarchical data, and it is used with components such as the `Ext.dataview.NestedList`, used in the framework to represent nested sets of information.

Stores depend, in turn, of *Proxies*. These are instances of the `Ext.data.proxy.Proxy` class (or its subclasses), and they encapsulate the logic required for a particular storage technology. For example, there are proxies for the following types of storage:

`Ext.data.proxy.Ajax`

Allows the application to talk to a backend server, using the common CRUD methods. This is one of the most important proxies available; developers can customize them in many ways, like specifying the URLs for each of the API operations, and to pass parameters for each of those operations. A subclass of this proxy, `Ext.data.proxy.Rest` is specifically tailored for connecting to REST services.

`Ext.data.proxy.JsonP`

Another type of server-bound proxy, like the `Ext.data.proxy.Ajax` class; in this case, this proxy is able to read data from domains other than that of the original web application.

`Ext.data.proxy.Memory`

Stores data in an in-memory array, lost when the page is refreshed or when the user navigates away from the page.

`Ext.data.proxy.LocalStorage` *and* `Ext.data.proxy.SessionStorage`
> Allow developers to store data in, you guessed it, the new HTML5 standard storage mechanisms.

Finally, server-bound proxies depend in turn on *writers* and *readers*. These classes, respectively located in the `Ext.data.writer` and `Ext.data.reader` namespaces, provide serialization and deserialization mechanisms for creating and reading XML, JSON payloads. Readers and writers are usually tied to server-bound proxies.

In our sample application, we are going to use a simple local storage proxy, which does not require a reader or a writer.

The Data Model

Sencha Touch uses the MVC architecture throughout its system. It allows developers to separate clearly the model classes from the view logic. It also allows developers to create adhoc stores, local or remote, to read and write those model instances.

In this sample, we are first going to write the application all in the same JavaScript file, and then we are going to separate the different elements in different files.

The first thing we are going to do in our app is to describe the model and the store where the model instances will be stored. This is the definition of a model class:

```
Ext.define('ToDoListApp.model.Task', {
    extend: 'Ext.data.Model',
    config: {
        fields: [
            {
                name: 'id',
                type: 'int'
            }, {
                name: 'completed',
                type: 'boolean'
            }, {
                name: 'dueDate',
                type: 'date'
            }, {
                name: 'title',
                type: 'string'
            }, {
                name: 'description',
                type: 'string'
            }],
        idProperty: 'id'
    }
});
```

As you can see, you can define all the characteristics of a Task, including the type and default values of each of its properties. In our case, a Task is defined by a numeric ID, a name, a description (both textual), a boolean value (stating whether the task has been done or not), and a due date.

Finally, we are specifying a proxy for our model, which provides the information of the location of the data. In this case we will be using the `localStorage` proxy, which means that the data will be stored as JSON objects in the HTML5 `localStorage` container of the browser.

Then we will specify a store for the model. A Sencha Touch store creates an intermediate object between your application controllers and the data they manage, allowing to provide information used to display the data in a meaningful way, such as its order or its grouping. In the case of our application, we are going to define the following Store:

```
Ext.define('ToDoListApp.store.TaskStore', {
    extend: 'Ext.data.Store',
    requires: [
        'ToDoListApp.model.Task'
    ],

    config: {
        model: 'ToDoListApp.model.Task',
        sorters: [{
            property: "dueDate",
            direction: "ASC"
        }],
        autoLoad: true,
        autoSync: true,
        singleton: true,
        storeId: 'TaskStore',
        proxy: {
            type: 'localstorage',
            id: "senchatasks"
        },
        grouper: function(record) {
            if (record && record.get("dueDate")) {
                return record.get("dueDate").toDateString();
            }
        }
    }
});
```

Creating the List

The first screen of our application is, of course, the list of tasks. In this screen we will display all the current tasks available, and whenever the application launches, it will synchronize the items available in the local database and display them:

```
Ext.define('ToDoListApp.view.TaskList', {
    extend: 'Ext.dataview.List',
    requires: [
        'ToDoListApp.store.TaskStore'
    ],

    config: {
        displayField: 'title',
        id: 'taskList',
```

```
            store: Ext.create('ToDoListApp.store.TaskStore'),
            itemTpl: '<div class="task completed_{completed}">{title}</div>',
            onItemDisclosure: true,
            emptyText: '<p align="center" class="instructions">No tasks here yet.<br/>Tap
    the "+" button to create one.</p>',
            grouped: true,

            items: [{
                xtype: 'toolbar',
                title: 'To Do List',
                docked: 'top',
                ui: 'light',
                items: [{
                    xtype: 'spacer'
                }, {
                    xtype: 'button',
                    ui: 'plain',
                    iconCls: 'add',
                    iconMask: true,
                    text: '',
                    action: 'createTask'
                }]
            }]
        }
    });
```

This is a very simple `Ext.dataview.List` that we are defining here; it will use the data store defined above as source of its data, and we are defining some useful properties, such as the fact that it will be grouped, and that every item shown will use a template.

Item templates are a very useful feature of Sencha Touch lists; they allow us to define the internal structure of each cell, and they are very similar to templates created using the jQuery Template plug-in.

One of the most interesting parts of the cell template is the fact that we can specify the data fields of each task, and how they are shown, just by encapsulating them between curly brackets.

Creating a To Do Item Form

The list is the first screen of our application. We also want to be able to create, edit, and delete To Do items, and for that we are going to create a form:

```
Ext.define('ToDoListApp.view.TaskForm', {
    extend: 'Ext.form.Panel',

    config: {
        id: 'taskForm',
        items: []
    }
});
```

The `Ext.form.Panel` class is there to help us. As usual, it takes a dictionary object with configuration options, and in particular, it uses a titlebar and two fieldsets; each one of these fieldsets will be rendered as its own group; the first fieldset contains all the data fields required to define a To Do item (see Figure 4-4):

```
{
    xtype: 'fieldset',
    id: 'mainFieldSet',
    instructions: 'Enter the details of the task',
    title: 'Task Details',
    items: [{
        xtype: 'textfield',
        id: 'titleField',
        label: 'Title',
        name: 'title',
        autoCapitalize: true,
        placeHolder: 'Enter a title'
    }, {
        xtype: 'textareafield',
        id: 'descriptionField',
        label: 'Description',
        name: 'description',
        autoCapitalize: true,
        placeHolder: 'Enter a description'
    }, {
        xtype: 'datepickerfield',
        id: 'dateField',
        label: 'Due on',
        name: 'dueDate',
        placeHolder: 'dd/mm/yyyy',
        dateFormat: 'D d M Y',
        picker: {
            slotOrder: [
                'day',
                'month',
                'year'
            ],
            yearFrom: (new Date()).getFullYear(),
            yearTo: (new Date()).getFullYear() + 10
        }
    }, {
        xtype: 'togglefield',
        id: 'completedField',
        label: 'Done',
        name: 'completed'
    }]
}
```

Figure 4-4. Form to create to do items

The second fieldset is shown only when the form is used to edit an item, and contains a single Delete button (shown in Figure 4-5):

```
{
    xtype: 'fieldset',
    id: 'taskFormDeleteFieldset',
    instructions: 'This cannot be undone',
    title: 'Actions',
    items: [
        {
        xtype: 'button',
        height: 44,
        id: 'deleteButton',
        ui: 'decline',
        text: 'Delete this task',
        action: 'deleteTask'
    }
```

The `confirmAndDelete` method asks the user for a confirmation before deleting the file, as shown in Figure 4-6.

A Controller to Rule Them All

The missing piece in our discussion of the MVC paradigm is, as you might have guessed, the controller. In Sencha Touch, controllers are defined as subclasses of the `Ext.app.Con troller` class. They serve as the glue that ties models, stores and views together, and

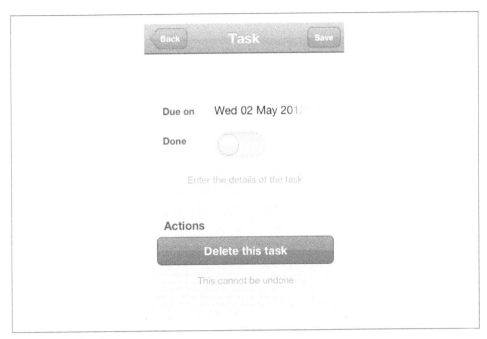

Figure 4-5. Delete button

they provide a handy mechanism allowing developers to centralize all their application logic in a single place.

This is a very basic definition of a controller:

```
Ext.define('ToDoListApp.controller.TaskController', {
    extend: 'Ext.app.Controller',

    config: {
        id: 'taskController',
        refs: {
            saveButton: 'button[action=saveTask]',
            taskForm: '#taskForm',
        },
        control: {
            saveButton: {
                tap: 'saveTask'
            }
        }
    },

    launch: function () {
        this.updateTaskCount();
    },

    saveTask: function (button, e, eOpts) {
        // ... the code to save a task ...
        var form = this.getTaskForm();
        // ...
```

```
      }
});
```

A typical Sencha Touch controller is composed of three main sections:

- A config object, itself containing two dictionaries:

  refs
  > Contain references to individual UI widgets anywhere in the application

  control
  > Defines, for each control, the event handlers that will be assigned.
- A launch function, which is called after the main application launch function, and which serves as a good initialization point for the application
- One or more event handling functions

Figure 4-6. Confirmation shown before removing an item

Let's analyze in detail how controllers work:

1. The refs collection mentions the existence of a button, whose action parameter is the string saveTask. There is also a reference to the task edition form, whose ID is taskForm. Sencha Touch controllers can reference widgets and controls using either of these syntaxes, making it very easy for developers to pinpoint individual components all over the application.

2. Later, in the control dictionary, we attach an event handler for the tap event on the button specified by the saveButton entry; the value of this event handler is a

string, which is exactly the name of the method in the controller that will be fired when the user touches the button.

3. Finally, the `saveTask` function contains the code that actually performs the requested action.

Another handy feature of the `refs` collection is that the controller will generate, automatically, getter methods that can be used to access individual components. For example, in the code above, the developer will be able to use the `getTaskForm()` method at any moment to retrieve a reference to that particular component.

Although nothing prevents developers from adding the event handling code directly in their views, controllers provide a handy and simple way to organize applications from the very beginning, allowing them to grow bigger and more complex as time passes.

Reacting to Events

There are many different event listeners that we can attach ourselves to, and the Sencha Touch documentation describes in great detail what is required for each one of them.

The most important listeners that you are going to use as a Sencha Touch developer are:

render
: Called when the panel is drawn on screen for the first time. There are similar `beforerender` and `afterrender` listeners that are useful for the developer.

activate
: Executed whenever the panel is active through the `setActiveItem` method.

itemtap
: Executed whenever an item in the list is tapped.

orientationchange
: As the name implies, this callback is executed after the device changes its orientation.

Each event requires a function with a particular signature; the Sencha Touch documentation describes in detail their structures.

The `saveTask` event handler in our controller has exactly the same parameters specified in the Sencha Touch documentation; you can find all of these parameters in their corresponding documentation, and it is strongly suggested to specify them all, even if the dynamic nature of JavaScript makes this an optional feature.

Navigation

How does the application navigate from one screen to the other? As you can see by yourself, the application allows you to follow a navigation pattern very similar to that of the UINavigationController class in iOS, where one screen is pushed after the other, and a Back button allows you to return to where you were.

However, in Sencha Touch there is no such thing as a navigation controller, and thus you must handle the navigation manually. In the case of the To Do List application, there are basically two transitions:

1. From the list to the form
2. Back from the form to the list

The first animation is triggered every time you touch the + button, or every time you select an item in the list. In both cases, the magic is created by using the setActiveI tem() method of the Panel class. This method accepts parameters that define the kind and direction of the transition to be used.

This method is called in the Viewport instance, which has two items: the list and the form. Our controller triggers the navigation, passing some parameters, as required by the user:

```
showForm: function() {
    Ext.Viewport.getLayout().setAnimation({
        type: 'slide',
        direction: 'left'
    });
    Ext.Viewport.setActiveItem(this.getTaskForm());
},

showList: function() {
    Ext.Viewport.getLayout().setAnimation({
        type: 'slide',
        direction: 'right'
    });
    Ext.Viewport.setActiveItem(this.getTaskList());
},
```

The viewport is just a panel, containing the list of to do items and a toolbar, and the second one is the task form. The setActiveItem() function is used to jump from panel to panel, creating the illusion of a transition between both.

The concept of the viewport is central to Sencha Touch, and this singleton object is a standard way to designate the root view that is visible at all times in the application. iOS developers can think of the viewport as the UIWindow instance where all the application is drawn and displayed.

Using Sencha Architect 2

As you have seen in this chapter, the creation of a Sencha Touch application uses a fairly descriptive, JSON-like structure of code. Developers use this to literally describe each and every detail of the user interface, and Sencha Touch allows them to organize this code in separate files for convenience.

The fact that most of the UI of a Sencha Touch application can be described with literal objects is one of the keys behind the success of the Sencha Architect 2[1], a commercial tool provided by the creators of Sencha Touch. Sencha Architect is very similar in nature to the visual builders found in products like Visual Basic or Xcode, allowing developers to create user interfaces with a mouse.

Sencha Architect 2 provides developers and designers for a common tool, integrated with a code generator, that can be used to create fully fledged applications in a very short amount of time. It uses the common canvas UI paradigm, with a widget palette on the left pane, a central editor canvas, and a project browser plus a properties pane on the left. The properties pane displays all the editable properties of the currently selected object on the canvas or on the project browser.

Figure 4-7 shows the tool running on OS X.

1. Previously known as Sencha Designer.

Figure 4-7. Sencha Architect 2

Sencha Architect 2 is a commercial application.

Sencha Architect 2[2] is available for Mac, Windows and Linux, with a commercial license; a preview version, valid for 90 days, can be downloaded for free. It can be used not only to create and edit Sencha Touch applications, but also Ext.js ones.

Conclusion

Sencha Touch is a very complex framework, and of course this chapter scratches only the surface of what can be done with it. Currently it is available in version 2.0, bringing

2. Sencha Architect 2 was in beta at the time of this writing.

several new features over 1.0, like a brazenly fast rendering engine (based in CSS, and thus, hardware-accelerated in iOS devices), and a new class system, which is 100% similar to the one available in ExtJS 4, much faster and easier to use.

However, Sencha Touch has the major drawback of not being available for non WebKit-based mobile browsers, which dramatically limits its cross-platform support. It compensates this fact by a tremendously polished UI, one that truly sets it apart from other mobile frameworks, and by a solid architecture, which makes it a serious alternative for enterprise software users.

CHAPTER 5

PhoneGap

The last framework we are going to see in this book is PhoneGap (*http://phonegap .com/*), an innovative system that allows developers to package web applications as native mobile apps.

PhoneGap was created by a company called Nitobi (*http://nitobi.com/*), which was acquired by Adobe. Furthermore, PhoneGap has become an official project of the Apache Foundation and it is called now Apache Cordova (*http://incubator.apache.org/projects/ callback.html*)[1]. Technically speaking, it can be said that *PhoneGap is a distribution of Apache Cordova*.

 At the time of this writing, the current stable version of PhoneGap is version 1.7.0.

Introduction

PhoneGap wraps applications created using HTML, CSS, and JavaScript into native applications, using the native web browser component provided by most native smartphone development toolkits.

As Adobe promotes it, PhoneGap is actually two things:

Wrapper
    PhoneGap takes your HTML, CSS, and JavaScript files and packages them in such a way that can be deployed to an online store.

Bridge
    PhoneGap also provides mechanisms to augment HTML5 web applications, allowing them to access and consume information and services otherwise available

---

1. You might also hear about PhoneGap being called "Apache Callback," and even the URLs at the Apache Foundation website say so; but Cordova is the official name to use from now on.

only to native applications, such as the local address book, the notification system, sounds, and other utilities.

Supported Platforms

At the time of this writing, PhoneGap currently supports the following mobile platforms:

- Apple iOS
- Android
- BlackBerry (since version 4.6, including the PlayBook)
- HP webOS
- Microsoft Windows Phone 7
- Symbian
- Bada

Supported Features

As a bridge, PhoneGap allows developers to access the following features:

- Accelerometer
- Address Book
- Camera
- Compass
- File system
- Geolocation
- Media
- Network
- Notifications
- Storage

Unfortunately, so far not all features are supported in all the mobile platforms in which PhoneGap runs; there is a chart available at the PhoneGap site (*http://phonegap.com/about/features*), reproduced in Figure 5-1, which shows the features available for each platform. However, as a rule of thumb, you can remember that *only iOS, Android, and Windows Phone 7 have full support for all of PhoneGap.*

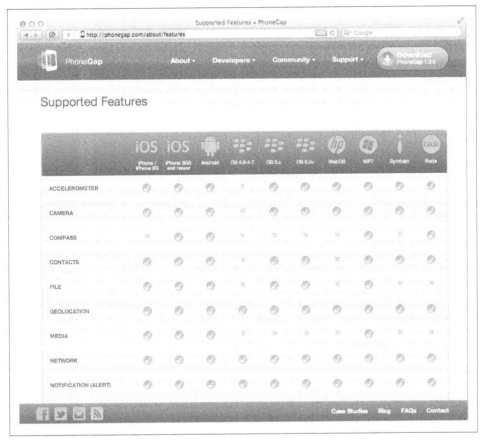

Figure 5-1. Supported PhoneGap features

Basic Usage

To create a native application using PhoneGap usually involves the following steps:

1. Create the web application you are going to package.
2. Install the PhoneGap framework in your development machine.
3. Create a PhoneGap application in your IDE.
4. Add the required HTML, CSS, and JavaScript files.
5. Build your application as you normally would, test, and deploy!

The following sections will show how to perform these steps to create iPhone and Android applications.

PhoneGap Build

Another interesting option is to use the PhoneGap Build (*https://build .phonegap.com/*) service, which makes developers' lives easier by just providing an upload and download model. This way, developers just upload their source code, and they can download binaries for various mobile platforms, ready to be signed, executed, and deployed.

Installing PhoneGap

The first step is to download the PhoneGap distribution, available from the Phone-Gap (*http://phonegap.com/*) home page, and to unzip its contents. Figure 5-2 shows the contents of the package, with subfolders for each supported mobile platform.

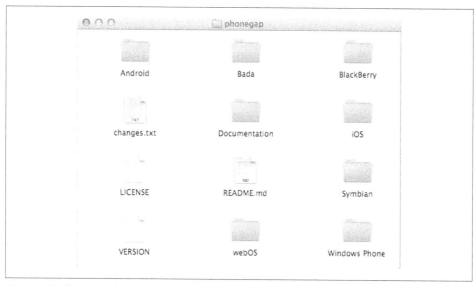

Figure 5-2. PhoneGap folder

In this chapter, we are going to see how to create packaged versions of the Sencha Touch and jQuery Mobile applications we created in the previous steps.

Creating an iOS Application

The iOS folder of the PhoneGap installation package contains the *PhoneGap-X.X.X.dmg* file. Opening that file will create a virtual disk on your desktop, and inside of it you will find the typical Mac OS X installer, as shown in Figure 5-3. Double-clicking that icon opens a wizard that helps you install PhoneGap on your Mac.

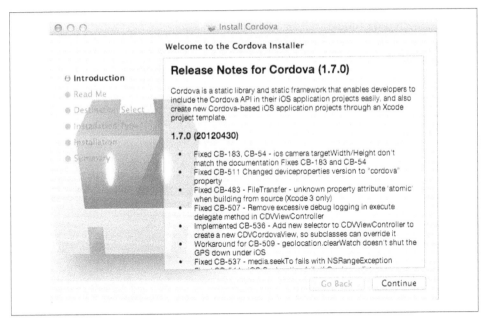

Figure 5-3. PhoneGap iOS installer

The PhoneGap for iOS installer requires the free iOS developer tools from Apple to be installed on your machine, so make sure you have them!

After you have executed the installer, Xcode will include a new Figure 5-4 called "PhoneGap-based Application." Create a new project of that kind, and save it on your desktop.

Now you need to add the required HTML files for your application, and the next step is probably the most tricky part of using PhoneGap, and a source of confusion for many new users of this tool:

1. Run the application, just like that. Empty. You will have a new www folder in your project folder after that.

2. First you have to add your HTML, CSS, and JavaScript files to the www folder created for you in the project folder (you can see that in Finder).

3. Then you have to add your www folder to your Xcode project as shown in Figure 5-5.

You might need to edit your HTML so that the proper libraries are referenced correctly. In our case, something like this will be enough:

```
<!DOCTYPE html>
<html>
    <head>
        <meta charset="utf-8" />
        <meta name="apple-mobile-web-app-capable" content="yes" />
```

```
<title>To Do List</title>

<script src="sencha-touch.js"></script>
<link href="sencha-touch.css" rel="stylesheet">

<link rel="stylesheet" href="style.css">
<script src="app.js"></script>

<link rel="apple-touch-icon" href="icon.png"/>
<link rel="apple-touch-startup-image" href="res/img/Default.png" />

        </head>
        <body></body>
    </html>
```

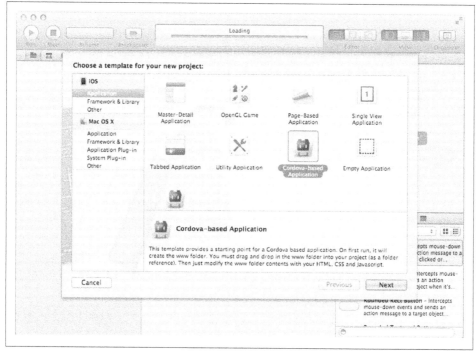

Figure 5-4. PhoneGap project template

The only thing that remains to be done is to select the "Product/Run" menu (or to hit the Command-R shortcut) and the web application will run inside of the iOS simulator, as a native application! From this point on, you can submit it to the App Store as any other application.

About That Bouncing Behavior in iOS Applications

Many iOS applications built with PhoneGap show a weird bug, which causes the whole application to bounce around as the user interacts with it. This is not very nice, and can be solved very easily setting the UI-WebViewBounce key to NO in the Cordova.plist file[2].

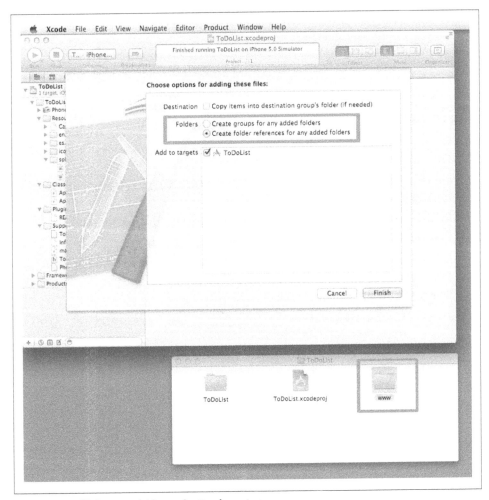

Figure 5-5. Add the www folder to the Xcode project

---

2. See Greg's Ramblings blog (*http://gregsramblings.com/2012/05/14/phonegap-howto-prevent -bounce-uiwebviewbounce/*).

Creating an Android Application

We are going to see how to create a native Android application using PhoneGap, both with Eclipse and with IntelliJ IDEA, which is a great alternative IDE to Eclipse.

 In this section, we assume that you have installed the latest Android toolkits in your development machine. Although the screenshots refer specifically to Mac OS X, the same steps should work in all platforms as well. The Android SDK can be downloaded freely from the official Android developer site (*http://developer.android.com/index.html*), while Eclipse can be downloaded also freely from the Eclipse Foundation site (*http://www.eclipse.org/*)[3].

With Eclipse

1. Open Eclipse and create a new project of type Android application, using the latest SDK and the default options.
2. Add two folders in Eclipse: `libs` and `assets/www`, by right-clicking and selecting New→Folder.
3. Copy the *phonegap-1.5.0.jar* file from your PhoneGap download to `libs`.
4. Copy the `xml` folder from the PhoneGap download to `res`.
5. Copy the contents `www` folder used in the Xcode section into your Eclipse project, under the `assets/www` folder.
6. Change the default activity of the project to the following:

```
package com.akosma.Savarasasa;

import android.os.Bundle;
import com.phonegap.*;

public class SavarasasaActivity extends DroidGap {
    /** Called when the activity is first created. */
    @Override
    public void onCreate(Bundle savedInstanceState) {
        super.onCreate(savedInstanceState);
        super.loadUrl("file:///android_asset/www/index.html");
    }
}
```

7. If after the previous step you still see errors, right-click on the `libs` folder and select Build Paths...→Configure Build Paths. In the dialog box that appears, select the Libraries tab and add the *PhoneGap.jar* file to the list.

8. Open the *AndroidManifest.xml* file and add the following under versionName:

---

3. At the time of this writing, the latest Android SDK is version 4 (SDK r15), and the latest Eclipse version is Eclipse Indigo (3.7.1).

Figure 5-6. Configure Eclipse build paths

```
<supports-screens
android:largeScreens="true"
android:normalScreens="true"
android:smallScreens="true"
android:resizeable="true"
android:anyDensity="true"
/>
<uses-permission android:name="android.permission.CAMERA" />
<uses-permission android:name="android.permission.VIBRATE" />
<uses-permission android:name="android.permission.ACCESS_COARSE_LOCATION" />
<uses-permission android:name="android.permission.ACCESS_FINE_LOCATION" />
<uses-permission
android:name="android.permission.ACCESS_LOCATION_EXTRA_COMMANDS" />
<uses-permission android:name="android.permission.READ_PHONE_STATE" />
<uses-permission android:name="android.permission.INTERNET" />
<uses-permission android:name="android.permission.RECEIVE_SMS" />
<uses-permission android:name="android.permission.RECORD_AUDIO" />
<uses-permission android:name="android.permission.MODIFY_AUDIO_SETTINGS" />
<uses-permission android:name="android.permission.READ_CONTACTS" />
<uses-permission android:name="android.permission.WRITE_CONTACTS" />
<uses-permission android:name="android.permission.WRITE_EXTERNAL_STORAGE" />
<uses-permission android:name="android.permission.ACCESS_NETWORK_STATE" />
<uses-permission android:name="android.permission.GET_ACCOUNTS" />
```

9. Add `android:configChanges="orientation|keyboardHidden"` to the activity tag in
   AndroidManifest.xml.

Figure 5-7. Final Eclipse project

10. Add a second activity under the application tag in AndroidManifest.xml:

```
<activity android:name="com.phonegap.DroidGap"
          android:label="@string/app_name"
          android:configChanges="orientation|keyboardHidden">
    <intent-filter>
    </intent-filter>
</activity>
```

Now you should be able to run your project (right-click on the project and select Run As→Android application). You should be prompted to use an Emulator or, if you plugged your device in, you should see the application running by now.

Beware of assets with folder names starting with an underscore!

When adding your own web apps to your *assets/www* folder, pay attention *not* to use leading underscores (_) in your folder names. There is a bug open since 2009 (*http://code.google.com/p/android/issues/detail ?id=5343*) that prevents assets to be packed during the build process if the name begins with an underscore.

With IntelliJ IDEA

IntelliJ IDEA (*http://www.jetbrains.com/idea/*) is a very interesting alternative to Eclipse when creating native Android applications, as a widely recognized as very capable commercial tool. Although IntelliJ IDEA is a commercial IDE, it is also available in a free community edition, suitable for learning and for the creation of open source software. We are going to use this version in this section [4].

1. Open IntelliJ IDEA and select "Create New Project" from the welcome screen, or select File→New Project... from the menu.
2. Select "Create new project from scratch."
3. Select "Android Module" from the type selector at the bottom, and enter a name and location for your project.
4. Create a source directory.
5. Select an Android SDK and create a default application structure.
6. Just like with Eclipse, add the PhoneGap jar file, XML files, and the web assets, in the same locations within the project. Perform steps 3 through 10, including the changes in all the source code files.
7. To configure the library dependency, right-click on the project and select "Open Module Settings." Select Modules, your application, and then click the "Dependencies" tab. Select PhoneGap and close the dialog boxes.
8. Select Run and your application should start the emulator.

Figure 5-8. Library configuration panel in IntelliJ IDEA

4. At the time of this writing, the latest available IntelliJ IDEA version was 10.5.2.

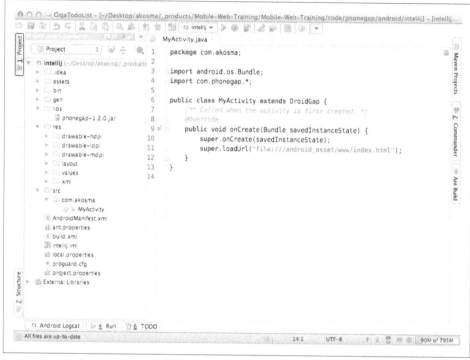

```
package com.akosma;

import android.os.Bundle;
import com.phonegap.*;

public class MyActivity extends DroidGap {
    /** Called when the activity is first created. */
    @Override
    public void onCreate(Bundle savedInstanceState) {
        super.onCreate(savedInstanceState);
        super.loadUrl("file:///android_asset/www/index.html");
    }
}
```

Figure 5-9. The final IntelliJ IDEA project

Creating a Windows Phone Application

The final platform we are going to install our web application in will be Windows Phone. Similarly to Xcode and iOS, the PhoneGap team has provided an excellent integration with Visual Studio Express, the IDE provided by Microsoft for free to create Windows Phone applications.

You can wrap your web application as a native Windows Phone application following these simple steps, which work on Windows Vista or Windows 7[5] with the Windows Phone SDK (*http://www.microsoft.com/download/en/details.aspx?displaylang=en&id= 27570*).

1. Copy the *CordovaStarter.zip* file included in the PhoneGap distribution into this folder: `C:\Users\[your username]\Documents\Visual Studio 2010\Templates\Proj ectTemplates\Visual C#` (or `Visual Basic` if you prefer to use this language).

2. Open Visual Studio and select File→New Project...

3. Select the "CordovaStarter" template.

---

5. Unfortunately, Visual Studio and the Windows Phone emulator do not work properly inside virtual machines, which means that you require a separate partition in your hard drive with Windows installed in it.

4. Include all the files of your web application (HTML, CSS, JavaScript, images, etc.) in the www folder of the Visual Studio project. These files have to be added as content.

5. Click on the famous green button that builds and runs applications in Visual Studio. Your application should be installed in the emulator automatically, and you should be able to use it right away.

6. If you want to deploy and run on a device, plug the smartphone to your computer, select "Windows Phone Device" in the drop-down menu next to the build and run button, and launch the executable.

How to test on a device?

Similarly, as with iOS, Microsoft requires Windows Phone developers to have an App Hub membership (*http://create.msdn.com/en-US/home/ membership*); at the time of this writing, such a membership costs USD 99 per year, which allows developers to submit up to 100 free applications, or an unlimited number of paying applications to the Windows Marketplace for Mobile (*http://www.windowsphone.com/en-US/market place*).

Accessing Native Functionality

We have mentioned at the beginning of this chapter that PhoneGap is both a *wrapper and a bridge*. So far we have learned how to wrap our applications, to create applications for different mobile platforms; now we are going to learn how developers can leverage the bridge, to access services provided for native applications.

Plug-ins

Another interesting characteristic of PhoneGap is that it has a plug-in architecture, which allows developers to provide custom functionality to their applications, wrapping accesses to native functionality that might not be available through PhoneGap. This requires the creation of a native code component *and* a JavaScript file, that will provide an extension of the bridge.

This architecture is pervasively used throughout PhoneGap, and the default distribution uses plug-ins thoroughly; for example, the Console plug-in, bundled with Phone-Gap, routes `console.log()` calls to the native console of the environment being used to run programs. This way, you can add logging calls in your web application and be able to follow their output in your favorite IDE.

This book will not provide more information about plug-ins, but you can check the standard PhoneGap documentation, which includes examples of how to create plug-ins.

The JavaScript Bridge

The magic behind the PhoneGap bridge is contained in the *cordova.js* file, provided in the PhoneGap distribution. The most important thing that you have to know about the PhoneGap JavaScript bridge library is that it overloads the `navigator` object with additional properties.

PhoneGap also provides a series of custom events, which we are going to see in the next section. Of all the events provided by PhoneGap, only a few are actually available in most platforms; in the section that follows we are only going to tackle those events that are available in as many platforms as possible.

The cordova.js file is platform-dependent?

Many developers have been puzzled in the past to learn that the *cordova.js* is different in every supported platform; some of them might even think that this is cheating, and that this breaks the cross-platform promise of PhoneGap. This is absolutely not true, because what actually matters is that each JavaScript file offers *the same interface* to your code! This means that you only have to write your application once, and thanks to PhoneGap, you can have it running in as many platforms as possible. Sounds cool, huh[6]?

So, remember: *each smartphone platform supported by PhoneGap has a different cordova.js file!*. This means that you cannot use the *cordova.js* file for Android in an iOS application, and so on.

In the latest version of PhoneGap (at the time of this writing, version 1.7), the Cordova team has included a unified version of the JavaScript bridge; from now on, the different files will slowly migrate to be one and the same. Check out this blog post introducing Cordova-JS (*http://phonegap.com/2012/03/21/introducing-cordova-js/*), the new technology that sets the roadmap for PhoneGap 2.0.

PhoneGap Kitchen Sink

To demonstrate the capabilities exposed by the PhoneGap bridge we are going to use an open source application created by Jens-Christian Fischer called the PhoneGap Kitchen Sink. This application is available on Github (*https://github.com/jcfischer/pgkitchensink*), and can be freely downloaded, used, and remixed as required. The code examples in the sections below will show fragments of this application.

The deviceready Event

PhoneGap provides an event that is fired when your web application is fully loaded inside the wrapper environment. This event is usually fired after the individual events

---

6. "Write once, run anywhere"; sounds familiar?

of other frameworks, like Sencha Touch or jQuery Mobile, so special care must be taken to ensure that these events are handled in the correct order.

Why is that? Because PhoneGap is not only a bridge, but also a wrapper; that means that the mobile web code could be ready to execute *before* the wrapper code is loaded, initialized, and ready to be used. This means that the JavaScript code could potentially call a service or function not yet ready in the native wrapper, and this could have very negative consequences. To remedy this, the PhoneGap wrapper infrastructure sends a deviceready event to the mobile application through the bridge; and this is how both the bridge and the wrapper are ready to work together.

The most basic use of the deviceready event is shown below. Just add an event listener to the current document, and you are done:

```
document.addEventListener("deviceready", initialize, false);

function initialize() {
    // Do something when the application is loaded in the device
}
```

You must always wait until the deviceready event is fired before wiring up other PhoneGap events. In the following sections, we are going to set up other event handlers inside of the initialize function, so that we are sure that everything is setup correctly.

However, if you are using frameworks such as jQuery Mobile, the respective startup functions might load in different order. In that case, you need to listen to both the load event, and then to the deviceready event:

```
window.addEventListener('load', function () {
    document.addEventListener('deviceready', function () {
        console.log("PhoneGap is now loaded!");
    }, false);
}, false);
```

When using version 2 of Sencha Touch, you do not need to worry about the device ready event. Sencha Touch 2 is aware of PhoneGap, and will wait until this event is fired to execute its own launch() function:

```
Ext.application({
    name: 'PhoneGapTest',
    launch: function() {
        // ... just as a normal Sencha Touch app, PhoneGap or not!
    }
});
```

Sencha Touch 1 and deviceready

Please pay attention to the fact that, while Sencha Touch 2 is aware of PhoneGap and will listen to the **deviceready** event, version 1 is not; and as such, you have to manually listen to both the **launch** and the **device ready** events, and manage the initialization of your application manually. Thankfully, this is no longer required since version 2 is available. If you need to use Sencha Touch version 1 with PhoneGap, please refer to the Sencha Touch tutorials site (*http://www.sencha.com/learn/legacy/ Tutorial:A_Sencha_Touch_MVC_application_with_PhoneGap:*) where the required steps are explained in detail.

Multitasking Events

Most smartphone platforms allow for multitasking these days; in those cases, whenever an application is opened while another is running, or when the user presses the Home button on their iOS devices, the application is usually put in an hibernating state, where the execution is stopped and where no touch events are sent.

PhoneGap provides two useful events for these situations: the function associated to the **pause** event is executed when the application is sent to the background, while the **resume** event is executed in exactly the opposite situation and when the application is brought again to the foreground.

The use of these events, as always, is as simple as it could be:

```
document.addEventListener("deviceready", initialize, false);

function initialize() {
    document.addEventListener("pause", sendToBackground, false);
    document.addEventListener("resume", bringToForeground, false);
}

function sendToBackground() {
    // Do something when the application is sent to the background
}

function bringToForeground() {
    // Do whatever is required when the application is brought to the
    // foreground
}
```

These events are very useful in the case of games. For example, whenever the **pause** event is triggered, games should stop and save the current state of the game, which should be restored when the **resume** event is fired.

Network Connectivity Events

I travel a lot by train. In Switzerland, the rail network is really good and you can go pretty much anywhere without the need to use a car. But, given that this is a country in the mountains, there are tunnels everywhere; and, as good as the Swiss mobile networks are, it can be tricky to keep a phone communication on the train, as it goes from tunnel to tunnel, let alone keeping a live 3G connection.

It is, then, fundamental to be aware of the fact that mobile networks can come and go really easily. Many applications require a continuous connection, and for those situations, the online and offline events come in handy. They allow the developer to attach functions that, as usual, will be executed when the phone goes, you guessed it, online or offline:

```
document.addEventListener("deviceready", initialize, false);

function initialize() {
    document.addEventListener("online", setOnline, false);
    document.addEventListener("offline", setOffline, false);
}

function setOnline() {
    // Do something when the device has a network connection to the internet
}

function setOffline() {
    // Disable any automatic data reload mechanisms and rely on offline data
    // stores, like the localStorage; because now you are offline!
}
```

Pay attention to the fact that the online and offline events rely on rather unreliable mechanisms to detect the current network status of the current device; as a matter of fact, a device can be online (which usually means, having an assigned IP address and a routing connection) without a real connection to the Internet (which actually depends on many other factors, usually out of reach from the user).

So, whenever your device goes online, remember to add the proper fallback code, in case your network requests are dropped or fail to return the required information.

Battery Events

Beyond networking considerations, battery life is a major factor to consider in mobile applications. Having applications that are able to react positively to negative battery conditions is a strong selling point! To help us with that, PhoneGap exposes the batterystatus, batterylow, and batterycritical events.

The first event, batterystatus is fired when the level of charge of the battery changes. The second event, batterylow is fired when the level of the battery is below some threshold; this threshold is defined by the host operating system. Finally, batterycritical is fired later, when you really, really, really, should plug your device in as soon as possible.

The callback function assigned to the three events is given an object as parameter, and this object contains two properties:

- `level` is a number between 0 and 100, returning the percentage of charge of the battery

- `isPlugged` is a boolean, stating whether the current device is plugged to the mains socket or not

Let's see a bit of source code using these events:

```
document.addEventListener("deviceready", initialize, false);

function initialize() {
    window.addEventListener("batterystatus", onBatteryStatus, false);
    window.addEventListener("batterylow", onBatteryLow, false);
    window.addEventListener("batterycritical", onBatteryCritical, false);
}

function onBatteryStatus(info) {
    console.log("Level: " + info.level + " isPlugged: " + info.isPlugged);
}

function onBatteryLow(info) {
    alert("Battery Level Low " + info.level + "%");
}

function onBatteryCritical(info) {
    alert("Battery Level Critical " + info.level + "%\nRecharge Soon!");
}
```

Accelerometer

Most modern smartphones these days include an accelerometer; these sensors provide information about the current position of the device regarding the center of Earth, and its current inertial acceleration while in motion.

PhoneGap provides a unified API to accessing this information from your web application, something that can be done in HTML5 already (check Chapter 1 for more information).

The following code snippet shows how to access accelerometer information using the PhoneGap bridge:

```
function accelerated(acceleration) {       ❶
    console.log("acceleration: (" + acceleration.x + ", "
    + acceleration.y + ", "
    + acceleration.z + ")"
    + ") obtained at " + acceleration.timestamp);
}

function error() {
    console.log('accelerometer error');
}

document.addEventListener("deviceready", function() {
```

```
    navigator.accelerometer.getCurrentAcceleration(accelerated, error); ❷
  }, false);
```

❶ The accelerometer callback function receives an object as parameter, containing three values, x, y, and z, with the composing parameters of the acceleration vector. It also contains a `timestamp` object, with the Unix timestamp in which the measure was obtained (this information can be useful for testing and logging).

❷ This call will trigger the execution of the `accelerated` function every time a new measure of acceleration is available. This, of course, can cause a bit of a penalty hit; so you might want to use `watchAcceleration` instead, which provides control on the timing of the accelerometer callback and can reduce a bit the CPU consumption of the device, as shown in the following example:

```
var options = { frequency: 2000 }; ❶

var watcher = navigator.accelerometer.watchAcceleration(accelerated, error, options);
❷

// some time later...

navigator.accelerometer.clearWatch(watcher); ❸
```

❶ This is measured in milliseconds. In this case, we will be watching the acceleration every two seconds.

❷ This method takes the same parameters as the `getCurrentAcceleration` method shown in the previous example. It also takes an `options` object with a `frequency` parameter, specifying the time distance between measures.

❸ The `clearWatch` function blocks PhoneGap from executing the accelerometer callback functions.

As you can see, PhoneGap uses very similar, asynchronous patterns to access information from the host device.

Address Book

The address book is a central piece for every smartphone platform, and one that raises numerous eyebrows from the point of view of privacy. Developers are able to interact with the contacts stored in the device, search for them, list them, and request the details of any of them.

PhoneGap provides an extensive API, composed of a rather simple set of methods and a quite complex object model, required to access contacts from your application. You can basically do two things:

- Search for contacts using the `find` method
- Create new contacts, thanks to the `create` method

The complexity of this API lies in the number of objects that are involved in the API:

- Contact
- ContactName
- ContactField
- ContactAddress
- ContactOrganization
- ContactFindOptions
- ContactError

The interaction of all these objects make the contacts API one that is not immediately obvious to use. The code below, taken from the PhoneGap Kitchen Sink application, shows how to request the list of contacts stored in the application, how to populate a list with them, and then how to request individually each contact, as the user touches individual items in the list:

```
var options = new ContactFindOptions();
options.multiple = true; ❶
options.filter = ""; ❷
var fields = ["id", "displayName", "name"]; ❸
navigator.contacts.find(fields, function(contacts) { ❹

    var index = 0;
    var len = 0;
    var list = $('#contactslist'); ❺
    list.empty();
    for (index = 0, len = contacts.length; index < len; ++index) {
        var contact = contacts[index];
        var newLi = $('<li>');
        var newA = $('<a>');
        newA.append(contact.name.formatted);
        newLi.append(newA);
        newLi.on('tap', createTapHandler(contact)); ❻
        list.append(newLi);
    }
    list.listview('refresh');

}, null, options);
```

❶ The first thing you want to do in this example is to get the full list of contacts stored in the current device. For that, create an instance of ContactFindOptions, and set the multiple property to true. This is very important, as the default value of this property is false!

❷ Setting the filter parameter to an empty string makes sure that the whole list of contacts will be returned, without any filtering.

❸ Then, specify the fields that you want to return from the contacts database. As you can imagine, the fewer fields you request, the less memory your application will consume. You should specify here only the fields that you are actually going to need at a particular point in time.

❹ This callback function is executed when the contact database returns results to the application; it takes a contacts array, containing all the instances that have been found in the database.

❺ Finally, we take the <ul> list in the HTML file and we will populate it with <li> elements, each showing the name of a contact.

❻ We are going to see the definition of this method later on. Suffice to say that it returns a function that is executed when the user taps on a particular item on the list.

One of the first observations when using the find() method is that the results are not ordered in any particular way; this means that we have to order them, manually, in memory. This, of course, can be a quite time-consuming operation in JavaScript:

```
contacts.sort(function (a, b) {
var an = a.name.formatted;
    var bn = b.name.formatted;
    return an == bn ? 0 : (an > bn ? 1 : -1);
});
```

The final operation is to provide a tap handler to every <li> in the list. This means that we are going to implement the createTapHandler shown in the previous example. This function returns a function, acting as a closure, keeping the value passed as parameter inside of the loop:

```
var createTapHandler = function(contact) {
    return function () {
        var opts = new ContactFindOptions();
        opts.multiple = false; ❶
        opts.filter = contact.id.toString(); ❷
        var fields = ["id", "displayName", "name", "emails", "phoneNumbers"]; ❸
        navigator.contacts.find(fields, function(contacts) {
            var person = contacts[0];
            $.mobile.changePage('#contactdetail');

            var data = [];
            data.push(person.name.formatted);
            // ...
```

❶ This time, we want only one instance returned from the contacts database.

❷ We pass as a filter the id parameter of the contact passed as parameter; pay attention to the fact that this parameter must be a string, or you could have crash in your code later on!

❸ We also specify more fields, as we want to display more information about the selected contact.

As you can see, the interaction among the different elements is a little bit more complex than in other PhoneGap APIs, but the end result is quite impressive. We are able to get information from the local contacts database, and interact with it and inspect it. Of course, this raises numerous red flags in terms of privacy and security, but used wisely, it is without a doubt a powerful feature to count on.

Many differences among platforms

The PhoneGap Contacts API depends on the underlying data model of contacts, as implemented by every platform. This has the consequence of a greater number of differences and incompatibilities among platforms, compared to other simpler APIs. Pay attention to all the different quirks documented in the official Contacts API documentation page (*http://docs.phonegap.com/en/1.5.0/phonegap_contacts_contacts.md .html#Contacts*).

Audio Recording and Playback

Modern smartphones are incredible machines, including microphones and speakers accessible to developers, to include useful recording and playback capabilities to their applications. Thankfully, PhoneGap includes APIs that allow us to access this hardware components, regardless of the underlying platform.

To record sound, and then to play it back immediately after the recording, we are going to need a very simple user interface, consisting of three buttons: one for starting the recording, one for starting the playback, and one to stop any operation in process. Let's define the code that will interact using those buttons:

```
var soundFile = null;
var recording = false;
function failure(error) {
    console.log('error: ' + error.code + ', message: ' + error.message);
}

function success() {
    console.log('media ready - success');
    $('#recordButton').show();
    $('#stopButton').hide();
    $('#playButton').show();
}

$('#recordButton').hide();
$('#stopButton').hide();
$('#playButton').hide(); ❶

var path = 'recording.wav';
window.requestFileSystem(LocalFileSystem.PERSISTENT, 0, function (fileSystem) { ❷
    fileSystem.root.getFile(path, {create: true}, function (fileEntry) { ❸
        soundFile = new Media(fileEntry.fullPath, success, failure); ❹
        $('#recordButton').show();
    }, failure);
}, failure);
```

❶ Set up the user interface properly upon initialization.

❷ iOS requires the file to exist before starting a new recording; so here you request the local filesystem, in order to...

---

❸ ...create a file. When that file is ready to be used...

❹ ...You create a Media object, with the requested path.

Let's add now some quite straighforward code to our buttons. First, the record button:

```
$("#recordButton").on('click', function (event) {
    if (soundFile) {
        $('#recordButton').hide();
        $('#stopButton').show();
        $('#playButton').hide();
        recording = true;
        soundFile.startRecord();
    }
});
```

Then, the play button:

```
$('#playButton').on('click', function (event) {
    if (soundFile) {
        $('#recordButton').hide();
        $('#stopButton').show();
        $('#playButton').hide();
        recording = false;
        soundFile.play();
    }
});
```

And finally, the code of the stop button. Just check the value of the `recording` flag to be sure what to stop!

```
$('#stopButton').on('click', function (event) {
    if (soundFile) {
        $('#recordButton').show();
        $('#stopButton').hide();
        $('#playButton').show();
        if (recording) {
            soundFile.stopRecord();
            recording = false;
        }
        else {
            soundFile.stop();
        }
    }
});
```

The PhoneGap audio API not only provides the functions shown above, but it also allows applications to know the current position of a `Media` object, thanks to the `getCurrentPosition()` method. Finally, the `getDuration()` method returns the length in seconds of the current instance.

A very important thing to keep in mind when working in Android: remember to call release on the Media file. This is actually required for Android, to release all in-memory handles to the Media file.

Camera

I remember back in 2002 when I bought my first cellphone with a camera; it was an Ericsson device, and frankly the camera was not as good as I expected it to be. Even worse, connecting to the device to get the images in my computer, or even trying to send them via email was an impossible task. Needless to say, I never actually used the camera in that device for anything useful. In 2005, I got a Motorola phone, and things were not any better.

It all changed with my first iPhone in 2008. I finally had a decent camera in my favorite smartphone, and not only that, loading those shots to my computer was as easy as plugging in the USB cable and launching iPhoto. Even better, a set of APIs allowed applications to consume images taken by the camera, which spawned a new hobby called "iPhoneography" (*http://www.iphoneography.com/*).

Things had finally changed.

PhoneGap offers a quite extensive, yet extremely minimalist interface for accessing the camera and the local photo library of the current user from any web application:

```
var options = {  ❶
    quality: 50,  ❷
    destinationType: Camera.DestinationType.DATA_URL,  ❸
    sourceType: Camera.PictureSourceType.CAMERA,  ❹
    allowEdit: false,  ❺
    encodingType: Camera.EncodingType.JPEG,  ❻
    targetWidth: 100,
    targetHeight: 100,
    mediaType: Camera.MediaType.PICTURE  ❼
};

function imageReady(imageData) {  ❽
    var img = document.getElementById('imgObject');
    var mimeType = 'image/jpeg';
    if (options.destinationType === Camera.DestinationType.DATA_URL) {
        if (options.encodingType === Camera.EncodingType.PNG) {
            mimeType = 'image/png';
        }
        img.src = 'data:' + mimeType + ';base64,' + imageData;
    }
    else if (options.destinationType === Camera.DestinationType.FILE_URI) {
        img.src = imageData;
    }
}

function imageError(message) {
    console.log(message);
}

document.addEventListener("deviceready", function() {
    navigator.camera.getPicture(imageReady, imageError, options);
}, false);
```

❶ This object actually wraps all the complexity of the camera manipulation.

❷ The quality parameter determines the final crispness of the resulting image. In the case of the iPhone, to avoid memory warnings, it is recommended to set this value at around 50.

❸ The possible values are DATA_URL and FILE_URI. The former provides the actual binary data from the image to the callback, in Base64 format; the latter only provides the path to the file in the local filesystem. When used in the iPhone, the FILE_URI option returns a path to the temporary directory of the current app, as the image is copied to that folder after the selection process. This folder is cleared when the application exits!

❹ The possible values are CAMERA, PHOTOLIBRARY, and SAVEDPHOTOALBUM. In the case of Android, both PHOTOLIBRARY and SAVEDPHOTOALBUM show the same photo album.

❺ Setting this to true displays an edition screen, allowing the user to crop, resize, and modify the image before it is sent to the application. This parameter works only on the iPhone, actually; all other platforms ignore it.

❻ Valid values are JPEG and PNG. Pay attention to set the correct MIME type of the image when using the DATA_URL destination type!

❼ The allowed parameters are CAMERA, VIDEO, and ALLMEDIA. The values speak for themselves. Of course, if you select the VIDEO option, given the potential size of the resulting object, the destinationType will be set automatically to FILE_URI.

❽ This callback receives a parameter whose nature depends on the options passed to the getPicture function.

Differences among platforms

Pay attention to the fact that the behavior of the getPicture() function change a lot from one platform to the other. You should always check the Quirks section at the end of the corresponding PhoneGap documentation page (*http://docs.phonegap.com/en/1.5.0/phonegap_camera _camera.md.html#Camera*) before attempting any integration in your own code, as every single smartphone platform reacts differently to this command.

Connection Status

Mobile networks are, by definition, unreliable; one second you are online, and the next, you are offline. Hence, mobile applications have to be able to detect, at any given time, the current status of the network connection, and be able to adapt their behavior accordingly. It is not the same to download a file through a WiFi or a GPRS connection, not at all.

We have seen previously how PhoneGap allows your application to know whether you are online or not; we have also seen how HTML5 allows any web application to know, at any given time, whether the device is connected or not[7]. PhoneGap also provides a very simple API that allows applications to know the quality of the current network connection of the device:

```
document.addEventListener('deviceready', function () {
    var networkState = navigator.network.connection.type;

    var states = {
        Connection.UNKNOWN: 'Impossible to know',
        Connection.ETHERNET: 'Ethernet',
        Connection.WIFI: 'Wifi',
        Connection.CELL_2G: 'Cellular 2G',
        Connection.CELL_3G: 'Cellular 3G',
        Connection.CELL_4G: 'Cellular 4G',
        Connection.NONE: 'No connection at all'
    };
    console.log('Current connection: ' + states[networkState]);
}, false);
```

Filesystem

We have briefly seen an example of use of the filesystem capabilities of PhoneGap in "Audio Recording and Playback" on page 112. The Filesystem API, similarly to the Address Book API, is rather complex and contains a large number of objects interacting with each other. Working with it is easy once you understand some core concepts.

To begin with, it is very important to remember that accessing the filesystem can be a very slow operation, particularly given the layers of abstraction between the operating system and the application, itself written in JavaScript and running in an embedded browser. To overcome this situation, and to make sure that the application stays responsive, PhoneGap uses an asynchronous approach for any functionality exposed by this API.

Let's start by writing some text into a new file.

The first thing we are going to do is to request an instance of the FileSystem class, through the requestFileSystem() function:

```
var fileSystem = null;

window.requestFileSystem(LocalFileSystem.PERSISTENT, 0, function (fs) { ❶
    fileSystem = fs;
    $('#createFileButton').show();
}, failure);
```

❶ The LocalFileSystem enumeration has two values: PERSISTENT is a reference to the area reserved for user files, that can be removed only if the user gives her consent;

---

7. Albeit, with some limitations, due particularly to the fact that network connectivity detection heuristics are inherently unreliable.

and TEMPORARY, which refers to the location where temporary files are stored. In this case, we want to create a permanent file.

The next thing to do is to call the getFile() function on the fileSystem object passed to the previous callback:

```
fileSystem.root.getFile(path, {create: true}, function (fileEntry) {  ❶
    console.log('file got');
    fileEntry.createWriter(function (writer) {
        // ... get some text to write here...  ❷

        writer.onwriteend = function (evt) {  ❸
            console.log('file written!');
        };
        writer.write(selectedText);  ❹

    }, failure);
}, failure);
```

❶ We call the getFile() function on the root of the fileEntry object we got in the previous code.

❷ We request a new FileWriter object, calling the createWriter() function of the fileEntry object, and when we get it, this callback is executed.

❸ We set up a function that will be called as soon as the contents of the file have been written, in the onwriteend event.

❹ And then we trigger the write() function, passing as parameter whichever text we want to write.

Now, let's read a file.

The operation required to read a file back in memory is very similar (and equally convoluted). We are going to create a FileReader object and we are going to wait for the text to be loaded, asynchronously, in the context of our application:

```
fileSystem.root.getFile(path, {create: true}, function (fileEntry) {
    fileEntry.file(function (file) {  ❶
        var reader = new FileReader();  ❷
        reader.onloadend = function(evt) {
            var text = reader.result;  ❸
        };
        reader.readAsText(file);  ❹
    }, failure);
}, failure);
```

❶ We have to call the file() function on the fileEntry object to get a reference to the underlying File object. Yes, there is a FileEntry class and a File class, and the former contains an instance of the latter. Not very obvious at first glance.

❷ We create a new FileReader instance here...

❸ ... which will return the contents of the text...

❹ ... after we trigger the execution of the `readAsText()` method.

For binary files, there is a similar `readAsDataURL()` function, which returns the contents of the file as a Base64-encoded string.

Now let's see some file information.

To request metadata from the file, we can use the same `File` object we requested in our last example:

```
fileSystem.root.getFile(path, {create: true}, function (fileEntry) {
    fileEntry.file(function (file) {
        var data = [
            'Full path: ' + file.fullPath,
            'MIME type: ' + file.type,
            'Modified on: ' + file.lastModifiedDate,
            'Size: ' + file.size
        ];
        var info = data.join('<br>');
        // show this data to the user somehow!
    }, failure);
}, failure);
```

And finally, a similar operation will allow us to remove the file from disk:

```
fileSystem.root.getFile(path, { create: true }, function (fileEntry) {
    console.log('file got, ready to be removed');
    fileEntry.remove(function() {
        console.log('file removed!');
    }, failure);
}, failure);
```

All file operations are asynchronous!

As you have seen in the preceding examples, all file operations are asynchronous. Remember to always pass your success and failure callback functions, to be notified of any situation. If you do not have a failure callback, your code will fail silently without providing any information to you, and this will most likely bring you some new white hair. And you do not want that!

Location and Compass

Arguably one of the most popular features of modern smartphones is undoubtedly the integration of a GPS chip. This single innovation has opened the door to countless innovations, from applications that allow users to share their current position with their friends, to others that allow them to track their daily jogging exercises.

Accessing the location information from a PhoneGap application is very simple, and is supported in nearly all platforms these days. As usual, the process involved is asynchronous, which means that your application will set a handler callback that will be executed as soon as the location information is returned from the device.

Emulating the HTML5 APIs

Readers familiar with the standard HTML5 APIs defined with the W3C have surely seen that their PhoneGap counterparts are very similar; this is not a secret, as the team behind PhoneGap has strived to keep a maximum level of compatibility with the HTML5 standard. The idea behind this is that, when browsers will implement these native APIs (Files, Media, Contacts, etc.) then their code will still work. In a certain sense, betting in PhoneGap is betting in the future.

```
var watchID = null; ❶

function startWatch() {
    var options = { maximumAge:3000, timeout:5000, enableHighAccuracy:true }; ❷
    watchID = navigator.geolocation.watchPosition(positionChanged, positionError,
options);
}

function stopWatch() {
    if (watchID) {
        navigator.geolocation.clearWatch(watchID);
        watchID = null;
    }
}

function positionChanged(position) { ❸
    lat = position.coords.latitude;
    lon = position.coords.longitude;
    alt = position.coords.altitude;
    accuracy = position.coords.accuracy;
    alt_accuracy = position.coords.altitudeAccuracy;
    heading = position.coords.heading;
    speed = position.coords.speed;
    timestamp = position.timestamp;
    // ...
```

❶ This variable will be used to store the result of the `watchPosition()` function, which will be used to call the `clearWatch()` function later.

❷ This object provides parameters for the `watchPosition()` function.

❸ Finally, the `position` parameter passed to the success callback contains all the information requested to the localization subsystem; you can use them in your application now.

Accessing the information provided by the compass is also very straightforward, requiring just a couple of lines of code:

```
var watchID = null; ❶

function startWatch() {
    var options = { frequency:200 }; ❷
    watchID = navigator.compass.watchHeading(headingChanged, headingError, options);
}
```

```
function stopWatch() {
    if (watchID) {
        navigator.compass.clearWatch(watchID);  ❸
        watchID = null;
    }
}

function headingChanged(heading) {
    $('#compass #heading').html(Math.floor(heading.magneticHeading));
    var rotation = "rotate(" + (360 - heading.magneticHeading) + "deg)";  ❹
    $('#compass #compass_img').css('-webkit-transform', rotation);
}
```

❶ We are going to use this variable to store a handle to the object returned by the watchHeading() function.

❷ Here we set some parameters for the watchHeading() function.

❸ The watchID object can be used to stop the updating operation; once the watch is cleared, the callback functions are not called anymore.

❹ The trick here consists in creating a WebKit rotation transformation, and to do this live as the device is moving around.

Notifications

PhoneGap provides a very simple API to create and display dialog boxes, to provide sound and vibration feedback to the user, to signal unusual situations, and to get the attention of the user when required.

If you want to show a native alert dialog box, you can use the code below. You can even provide a callback function that will be executed after the dialog box is closed:

```
document.addEventListener('deviceready', function () {
    var message = "This is a message for the user";
    var title = "This is the title of the dialog box";
    var button = "Close";  ❶
    navigator.notification.alert(message, callback, title, button);
}, false);

function callback() {
    console.log('The dialog box has been dismissed');
}
```

❶ The value by default is "OK"; this argument is ignored by Windows Phone 7.

If you want to ask a question to the user, you can use the following code:

```
document.addEventListener('deviceready', function () {
    var message = "This is a message for the user";
    var title = "This is the title of the dialog box";
    var buttons = "Yes, No";  ❶
    navigator.notification.confirm(message, callback, title, buttons);
}, false);
```

```
function callback() {
    console.log('The dialog box has been dismissed');
}
```

❶ The value by default is "OK, Cancel"; this argument is ignored by Windows Phone 7.

Finally, if you need to play a sound or to trigger a vibration in the device, you can use the following code:

```
document.addEventListener('deviceready', function () {
    navigator.notification.beep(4); ❶
    navigator.notification.vibrate(3000); ❷
}, false);
```

❶ The argument of the beep function is ignored by iOS. The sound that is played depends on the mobile platform where the application is running. In Android the sound is predefined in the settings. In iOS, there is no default sound, and the application should provide a file named *beep.wav*, whose playback time is no longer than 30 seconds. PhoneGap includes a standard beep sound for Windows Phone 7.

❷ The argument of the vibrate function is ignored by iOS.

Storage

PhoneGap provides a wrapper API that mimics the standard HTML5 storage APIs:

- localStorage
- sessionStorage
- SQLite databases

In those platforms where these APIs are not provided, PhoneGap provides an implementation that provides the same interface and implementation as specified by the W3C. We are not going to spend much time in these, since the Chapter 1 provides an extensive discussion about localStorage and sessionStorage.

The code below shows how to store values with each of these technologies; with the localStorage and the sessionStorage this is quite trivial:

```
window.localStorage['someString'] = selectedText;
window.sessionStorage['someString'] = selectedText;
```

With SQLite databases, the API is slightly more complex:

```
function populate(tx) {
    tx.executeSql('DROP TABLE IF EXISTS RANDOMTEXT');
    tx.executeSql('CREATE TABLE IF NOT EXISTS RANDOMTEXT (id unique, data)');
    tx.executeSql('INSERT INTO RANDOMTEXT (id, data) VALUES (1, \"' + selectedText +
'\")');
}

function error(err) {
```

```
        console.log('error: ' + err.code + ', message: ' + err.message);
    }

    function success() {
        console.log('database OK');

        // ... and here you should update your UI
    }

    // Now store the same data in a SQL database
    var db = window.openDatabase('database', '1.0', 'PGKitchenSink', 200000);
    db.transaction(populate, error, success);
```

To read data back from the localStorage and the sessionStorage is trivial, as usual:

```
window.localStorage['someString'] = selectedText;
window.sessionStorage['someString'] = selectedText;
```

To read data back from the SQLite database is slightly longer, but not very complex once you have understood how to work with databases:

```
function query(tx) {
    tx.executeSql('SELECT * FROM RANDOMTEXT', [], success, error);
}

function success(tx, results) {
    var length = results.rows.length;
    if (length > 0) {
        dbText = results.rows.item(0).data;
        console.log('text: ' + dbText);

        // ... and here you should update your UI
    }
}

var db = window.openDatabase('database', '1.0', 'PGKitchenSink', 200000);
db.transaction(query, error);
```

The success() callback function is called as soon as the transaction is finished, which can potentially take a long time (in CPU terms, that is). The second parameter of this function, results, contains all the rows returned by the database that correspond to the criteria of the query.

Conclusion

The most important thing to remember about PhoneGap is that it is both a *wrapper* and a *bridge*. Most applications are going to use PhoneGap as only a wrapper, since the bridge JavaScript files are optional. However, if you are going to use the JavaScript bridge, *remember to use the one that corresponds to the platform you are targeting!*

PhoneGap is an exciting technology, open source (it is licensed under the Apache License (*http://phonegap.com/about/license/*)) and now has the backing of an industry leader like Adobe. It has become a de facto standard, and it allows developers to reuse code across different mobile platforms, truly realizing the power of cross-platform development for mobile devices.

CHAPTER 6

Debugging and Testing

More than with any other programming language, the dynamic nature of JavaScript makes it fundamental to have the proper tools, in order to increase the quality of our applications. This chapter will provide an introduction to three very important tools used for debugging of mobile JavaScript applications: the WebKit Web Inspector, iWebInspector, and Adobe Shadow.

We are also going to see different techniques for testing your mobile applications. Of course, "testing" is a rather large concept, and it would be foolish to pretend that this short guide will give you a complete panorama of testing mobile web apps, but that is why this chapter is not called "Quality Assurance." However, simple testing techniques will allow you and your team to increase your productivity, providing working code in time and schedule.

Your Browser Web Inspector

The first tool that will be used to debug mobile web applications is the Web Inspector that ships natively with most modern browsers these days. It is a very powerful tool, originally inspired by the famous Firebug plug-in for Firefox by Joe Hewitt. These days, the WebKit Web Inspector, Opera DragonFly, or the Internet Explorer Developer Tools all allow you to perform the following functions:

- Inspect the HTML structure of the current web page, including all elements that are generated dynamically (this is specially handy in the case of Sencha Touch, which generates HTML elements on the fly).
- Set breakpoints in your JavaScript code, to debug your code and to verify that everything works as expected.
- Explore the different HTML5 storage options of your browser, including databases, cookies, or the `localStorage`.
- Modify the CSS of your page dynamically, changing properties and seeing them "live" on your page, which is a huge help for designers and developers alike.

Let's now explore some of these characteristics in detail.

Inspect the HTML of your app

Using the web inspector, you can see the complete structure of your page, including all the nested elements, and including those that are created during runtime. This is particularly useful when debugging the HTML code created by frameworks like Sencha Touch.

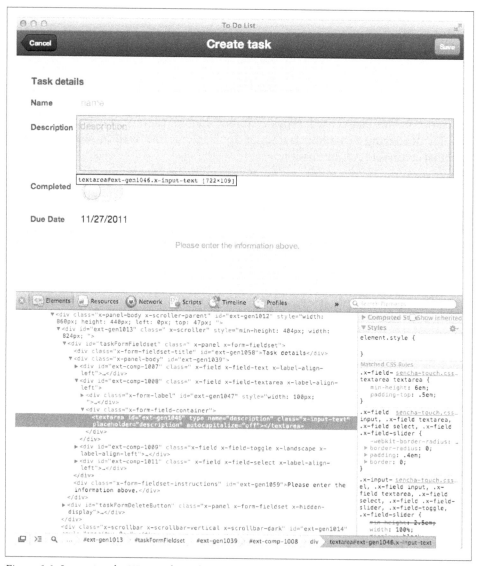

Figure 6-1. Inspecting the HTML of a mobile app

Log Messages in the Console

Using the console you can inspect the internal state of your application, without having to use the old alert() way of doing things. There are two different instructions that you can use to output text to the console:

console.log(message)
> When message is a string, this will output that text to the console. If the object is not a string, then the result of the toString() method will be called.

console.dir(object)
> Displays the complete structure of an object in the console, allowing you to see its internal tree structure.

 Some inspectors perform the same task when invoking console.log() and console.dir(); as always, there might be differences across browsers, however both methods are supported these days.

Set Breakpoints in Your JavaScript Code

Finally, the web inspector allows you to set breakpoints in your JavaScript code, which helps developers to execute their programs instruction by instruction, to see the values of the variables in the current stack frames, and to step in and out from functions, lambdas, and methods.

iWebInspector

The second tool we are going to talk about is iWebInspector (*http://www.iwebinspector .com/*), a tool for OS X that allows to inspect web applications running on the iOS Simulator (bundled with the free Xcode tools) as either fullscreen web apps, or in a PhoneGap container. This tool has been created by Maximiliano Firtman, well known in the mobile web development community as the author of several interesting books and very useful websites such as Mobile HTML5 (*http://mobilehtml5.org/*).

iWebInspector allows developers to use all the features of the WebKit web inspector from the simulator, thanks to a discovery made by Nathan de Vries (*http://atnan.com/ blog/2011/11/17/enabling-remote-debugging-via-private-apis-in-mobile-safari/*). You can load the inspector for any page running on Safari, any full screen web app saved on the home screen, or any PhoneGap application, and inspect all the internal state, just like with a normal browser.

Figure 6-2. Logging messages in the console

Adobe Shadow

As useful as the web inspector is, there are times when you would like to inspect the state of your application as it runs in a device or in the simulator; to help you with that, the Adobe Shadow (*http://labs.adobe.com/technologies/shadow/*) tool is there.

Figure 6-3. Setting breakpoints in JavaScript code

Adobe Shadow uses a project created originally by the PhoneGap team, called weinre (*http://phonegap.github.com/weinre/*) (this name stands for Web Inspector Remote). Adobe has taken weinre and has packaged it in a way that makes it very easy to use.

Adobe Shadow consists of the following elements:

- Desktop applications for Mac and Windows
- A Google Chrome plug-in
- Mobile applications for Android and iOS

To use Adobe Shadow, follow these steps:

1. Install the desktop application on the system of your choice.
2. Install the Google Chrome plug-in.
3. Install the mobile application in your device.
4. Launch the applications in both your computer and your smartphone or iPad.
5. Open a Google Chrome window, and navigate to the URL of your web application. Your mobile device should follow the navigation automatically, displaying (eventually) the mobile version, or at least the same page.
6. Launch your web application as you normally would, and use Adobe Shadow to inspect its internal state!

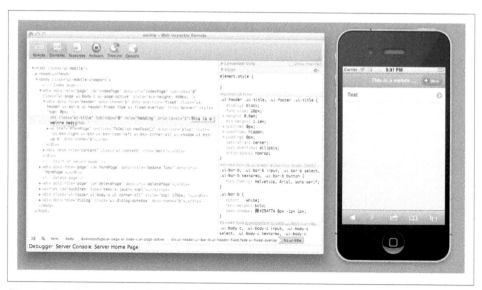

Figure 6-4. weinre session, including live DOM manipulation

Impressive, huh? This works on real devices over the network. At the moment of this writing, Adobe Shadow still does not allow for setting breakpoints and for executing JavaScript code step by step, but hopefully this functionality will be included soon.

Testing

This section will introduce one open source and one commercial testing frameworks that you can use to test your JavaScript applications:

- Jasmine (*https://github.com/pivotal/jasmine*)
- Siesta (*http://www.bryntum.com/products/siesta/*)

Jasmine

Test Driven Development (TDD) has probably been one of the major breakthroughs of the past 15 years. Nearly every programming language has at least one unit testing library, but lately the fashion has gone to the new field of Behavior Driven Development (BDD), in which the suite of tests will "describe" the actions taken by the piece of software being considered, evaluating the output against some predetermined values.

The idea behind BDD is not only to test the possible outcomes of a piece of software, but also to provide a living documentation that can be used by other developers or even by customers, to verify the correct mechanisms of their software.

Jasmine is a JavaScript BDD library that has two special characteristics to it. First, it does not require the DOM to work, which means that it is implemented using core JavaScript objects and APIs, and that Jasmine tests can run outside of the browser. The second interesting fact is that Jasmine does not depend on other libraries, which means that it's extremely simple to install and use. A suite of tests written with a BDD library is usually called a spec.

 The latest available version of Jasmine at the time of this writing is 1.2.0, with version 2.0 still in Release Candidate.

As a very simple example, let's use Jasmine to test a slightly modified version of the Task class used in the jQuery Mobile application described in Chapter 3. We are going to test the following class:

```
var Task = function () {
    var completed = false;
    var date = new Date();
    var name = "";
    var description = null;

    return {
        markAsDone: function() {
            completed = true;
        },

        resetDoneStatus: function () {
```

```
            completed = false;
        },

        isCompleted: function () {
            return completed;
        },

        setDate: function(newDate) {
            date = newDate;
        },

        getDate: function () {
            return date;
        },

        setName: function (newName) {
            name = newName;
        },

        getName: function () {
            return name;
        },

        setDescription: function (newDescription) {
            description = newDescription;
        },

        getDescription: function () {
            return description;
        }
    };
};
```

To do that, we have first to download the latest Jasmine library (*https://github.com/pivotal/jasmine/tags*) from Github. Inside the Jasmine distribution there is a lib/jasmine-core/example folder, containing a file named *SpecRunner.html*. We are going to modify that file and include our own classes:

```
<!DOCTYPE html>
<html>
<head>
<title>Jasmine Spec Runner</title>

<link rel="stylesheet" href="../jasmine.css">
<script src="Task.js"></script> ❶
<script src="TaskSpec.js"></script> ❷

<script>
(function() {
 var jasmineEnv = jasmine.getEnv();
 jasmineEnv.updateInterval = 1000;

 var trivialReporter = new jasmine.TrivialReporter();

 jasmineEnv.addReporter(trivialReporter);
```

```
jasmineEnv.specFilter = function(spec) {
    return trivialReporter.specFilter(spec);
};

var currentWindowOnload = window.onload;

window.onload = function() {
    if (currentWindowOnload) {
        currentWindowOnload();
    }
    execJasmine();
};

function execJasmine() {
    jasmineEnv.execute();
}

})();
</script>
</head>

<body>
</body>
</html>
```

❶ This file contains the definition of the class that we want to test.

❷ This file contains the spec files that describe the tests.

The spec file looks like a complete description of the behavior and structure of the class being tested. Jasmine provides functions named describe, inside containing several calls to a function called it:

```
describe ("Task", function() {
    var task = null;

    beforeEach (function() {
        task = new Task();
    });

    describe ("when a new one is created", function () {
        it ("should have an empty description", function () {
            expect(task.getDescription()).toBeNull();
        });

        it ("should have an empty name", function () {
            expect(task.getName()).toEqual("");
        });

        it ("should not be completed", function () {
            expect(task.isCompleted()).toBeFalsy();
        });
    });

    describe ("when one is modified", function () {
```

```
        it ("should have the specified completed status", function () {
            task.markAsDone();
            expect(task.isCompleted()).toBeTruthy();
        });
    });

    describe ("when one is reset", function () {
        it ("should not be marked as done", function () {
            task.resetDoneStatus();
            expect(task.isCompleted()).toBeFalsy();
        });
    });
});
```

Reloading the SpecRunner.html file on the browser provides the following output,
showing that all the tests have passed, and outputting the texts passed as parameters
of the describe and it functions. The result looks like shown in Figure 6-5.

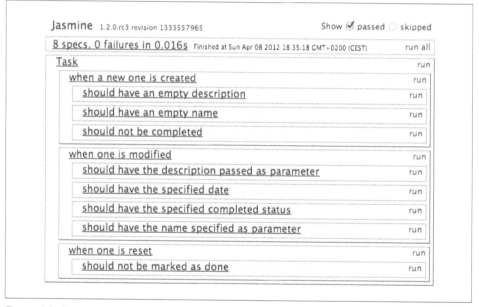

Figure 6-5. Jasmine output

> You can try Jasmine without installing it in your machine just by brows-
> ing to the Try Jasmine (*http://tryjasmine.com/*) site, created by the de-
> velopers of Jasmine.

Siesta

The final tool that we are going to introduce in this chapter is Siesta (*http://bryntum.com/products/siesta/*), a commercial testing framework that targets Ext.js and very recently also Sencha Touch applications.

Using Siesta, developers can automate integration testing tasks on their applications, simulating touches and navigation throughout their Sencha Touch app. They can be used to test not only individual components, but also whole applications, including the interaction between screens and the navigation.

Siesta is a product of Bryntum (*http://bryntum.com/*), a company in Helsingborg, Sweden started by Mats Bryntse (*https://twitter.com/bryntum*). Siesta is available in two versions: *Lite*, which is provided free of charge, and *Standard*, providing enterprise features like premium support, cross page testing, and Selenium (*http://seleniumhq.org/*) integration.

Siesta Standard unit test suites can also be executed on the command line, using PhantomJS (*http://phantomjs.org/*) or Node.js (*http://nodejs.org/*). This simplifies the integration of tests in larger, continuous integration chains.

We are going to show how to create a simple testing suite for our To Do List application, built with Sencha Touch 2 in Chapter 4.

The first thing we need to do is to create a bootstrap HTML and JavaScript file, that will be used to display the tests as they are executed:

```
<!DOCTYPE html>
<html>
    <head>
        <!-- Sencha Touch library CSS-->
        <link rel="stylesheet" href="../../_libs/sencha/resources/css/sencha-
touch.css">
        <title>Testing with Siesta</title>

        <!-- Siesta CSS -->
        <link rel="stylesheet" href="siesta-1.1.0-preview/resources/css/siesta-touch-
all.css">
    </head>
    <body>
        <div id="splashLoader">
            <div id="loading">
                <span class="loadTxt">Loading...</span>
                <div class="x-loading-spinner"><span class="x-loading-top"></span><span
class="x-loading-right"></span><span class="x-loading-bottom"></span><span class="x-
loading-left"></span></div>
            </div>
        </div>

        <!-- Sencha Touch library -->
        <script src="../../_libs/sencha/sencha-touch-all-debug.js"></script>

        <!-- Siesta application -->
```

```
                    <script src="siesta-1.1.0-preview/siesta-touch-all.js"></script>

                    <!-- The test harness -->
                    <script src="index.js"></script>
                </body>
            </html>
```

This HTML file references the Sencha Touch 2 and the Siesta libraries, each composed of a JavaScript and a CSS file.

The next step is to create a JavaScript file that will be used to describe the suite of tests to be executed:

```
var Harness = Siesta.Harness.Browser.SenchaTouch;

Harness.configure({
    title        : 'Testing the To Do List Application',
    transparentEx : false,
    loaderPath    : { 'ToDoListApp' : '/Sencha%20Touch/todoapp/app' }
});

Harness.start(
    {
        group : 'To Do List',

        // Load these files for each ST 2.0 test
        preload : [
            "/_libs/sencha/sencha-touch-all-debug.js",
            "/_libs/sencha/resources/css/sencha-touch.css"
        ],
        items : [
            'tests/sanity.js',
            'tests/model.js',
            'tests/createTask.js'
        ]
    }
);
```

Siesta requires various pieces of JavaScript code to define tests:

1. A "test harness," which will reference individual tests

2. One or more individual test files, each testing an individual section of the application

The configuration of the harness in the script above uses the loaderPath key, which is required by Siesta when dealing with MVC applications that use the Sencha Loader mechanism. We are providing, as a parameter, the location of the Sencha Application being tested.

Figure 6-6 shows the screen that is shown when the user navigates to the testing harness from within the Mobile Safari browser in an iOS device.

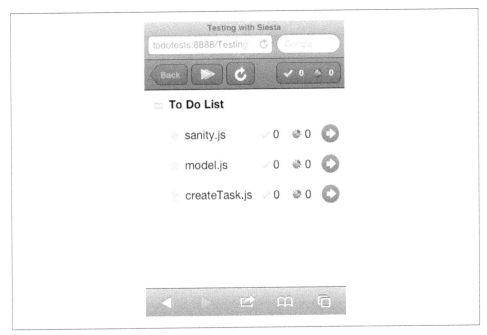

Figure 6-6. Siesta before executing the tests

Each individual testing file targets a particular aspect of the application being tested; for example, `tests/model.js` tests the `ToDoListApp.model.Task` class:

```
StartTest(function(t) {
    t.diag("Testing Task model");

    t.requireOk('ToDoListApp.model.Task', function() {
        var task = Ext.create('ToDoListApp.model.Task', {
            title: 'Buy milk',
            description: 'This is a test task',
            completed: true,
            dueDate: new Date()
        });

        t.is(task.get('title'), 'Buy milk', 'title works ok');
        t.is(task.get('description'), 'This is a test task', 'Could read description');
        t.ok(task.get('completed'), 'The task is completed');
        t.isNot(task.get('dueDate'), null, 'The task date must not be null');
    });
});
```

Siesta includes a number of useful assertions that can be used to test the state of different parts of the code:

`t.is()`
> Takes three parameters and verifies the identity or equality of the first two operands. As you might image, `t.isNot()` performs the inverse operation.

`t.ok()`

Verifies that a particular statement is `true`. Of course, `t.notOk()` does exactly the opposite.

Many other functions are provided by Siesta to allow developers to script the expected actions of their applications:

`t.requireOk()`

Used to load asynchronously required classes, and to perform a function once the code is loaded.

`t.chain()`

Used to execute a sequence of asynchronous operations, having Siesta waiting for the end of the current operation before starting a new one.

`t.waitForCQ()`

Expects a particular element to be rendered and available in the DOM before executing a callback function.

To see these functions in play, check the source code repository for this book. In the "Testing and Debugging" folder you'll find examples that cover these methods.

Figure 6-7 shows the iOS browser after all the tests have been executed. This screen details the number of tests that have been executed, including the number of failed and passed tests.

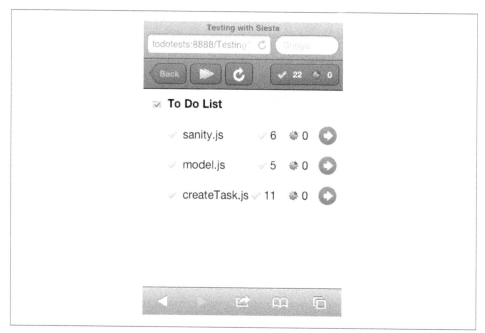

Figure 6-7. Siesta output after the execution of the tests

Developers can inspect the individual status of each test, as shown in Figure 6-8.

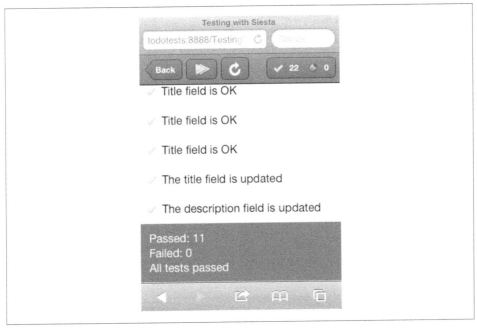

Figure 6-8. Result of an individual Siesta test

Conclusion

In this chapter, we saw how to use several different technologies to test our code before shipping it; some of them deal with the nitty-gritty details of your classes, testing their integrity and interfaces; others provide more advanced services, allowing you to script complex interactions and executing them in an automated fashion.

Both the Web Inspector and Adobe Shadow can be used to increase the quality of your applications. The former provides a solid debugging environment in which to execute code step by step, watching variables and setting breakpoints. On the other hand, Adobe Shadow provides an incredible new paradigm, allowing developers to inspect the internal state of their applications when running in their smartphone. This is invaluable when deploying web apps as native ones.

For Sencha Touch developers, Siesta brings an enterprise-level testing framework, which can be used to verify and certify the quality of any application.

Whatever the method that you use, do not forget that you should always have testers playing with your application, providing your team with feedback, and signalling potential problems to the developers. No matter how advanced your testing suite, you should always have human testers.

CHAPTER 7

Conclusion

Phew, what a ride! I hope that this book served as a good introduction to the world of modern mobile web app development.

Sencha Touch and jQuery Mobile are, at the time of this writing, the most serious options available. They both complement each other, providing software developers with serious options and an effective trade off:

Table 7-1. Comparison between Sencha Touch and jQuery Mobile

Library	Pros	Cons
Sencha Touch	Professional widgets	Webkit-only
	Complete toolkit	Heavyweight
	Enterprise-level support	Learning curve
	MVC Architecture	
jQuery Mobile	Broad browser support	Few widgets
	Lightweight	Younger code base
	Progressive enhancement	
	Easier to learn	

jQuery Mobile is dual licensed, with the MIT or GPL version 2; Sencha Touch is available under the GPL version 3 license for open source projects, and a paid commercial license for companies not willing to be subject to the terms imposed by the GPL.

Finally, using PhoneGap (or "Apache Cordova" as it is known now), developers can deploy their application not only through the web, but also in the corresponding marketplaces of several different mobile platforms.

All of these options turn mobile web apps in an extremely serious options, chosen by more and more companies and individuals every day for offering value added services and products. The tremendous evolution of the mobile web has made this a reality, and there is a bright future forward.

Bibliography

Books

[flanagan] David Flanagan. *JavaScript: The Definitive Guide, Sixth Edition (http://oreilly .com/catalog/9780596805531).* O'Reilly. 2011. ISBN 0-596-80552-7

[crockford] Douglas Crockford. *JavaScript: The Good Parts (http://oreilly.com/catalog/ 9780596517748).* O'Reilly. 2008. ISBN 0-596-51774-2.

[stefanov] Stoyan Stefanov. *JavaScript Patterns (http://shop.oreilly.com/product/ 9780596806767.do).* O'Reilly. 2010. ISBN 0-596-80675-2.

[firtman1] Maximiliano Firtman. *Programming the Mobile Web (http://oreilly.com/cat alog/9780596807795).* O'Reilly. 2010. ISBN 0-596-80778-3.

[firtman2] Maximiliano Firtman. *jQuery Mobile: Up and Running (http://shop.oreilly .com/product/0636920014607.do).* O'Reilly. 2012. ISBN 1-4493-9765-4.

[stark] Jonathan Stark. *Building iPhone Apps with HTML, CSS, and JavaScript (http:// oreilly.com/catalog/9780596805784).* O'Reilly. 2010. ISBN 0-596-80578-0.

[keith] Jeremy Keith. *HTML5 for Web Designers (http://www.abookapart.com/prod ucts/html5-for-web-designers).* A Book Apart. 2010. ISBN 978-0-9844425-0-8.

[cederholm] Dan Cederholm *CSS3 for Web Designers (http://www.abookapart.com/ products/css3-for-web-designers).* A Book Apart. 2011. ISBN 978-0-9844425-2-2.

Generic References about Mobile Web Technologies

Mobile HTML5 (*http://mobilehtml5.org/*)

Mobile Web Best Practices (*http://mobilewebbestpractices.com/*)

2011 in review: 20 HTML5 sites that changed the game (*http://www.netmagazine.com/ features/2011-review-20-html5-sites-changed-game*)

The Web Platform - Browser Technologies (*http://platform.html5.org/*)

When can I use... Support tables for HTML5, CSS3, etc (*http://caniuse.com/*)

Magic Quadrant for Mobile Application Development Platforms by Gartner (April 26th, 2012) (*http://www.gartner.com/technology/reprints.do?id=1-1AAE10P&ct= 120427&st=sb*)

Websites about HTML5

HTML5 Mobile Pro Download Edition (*http://html5mobilepro.com/*)

HTML5 Rocks (*http://www.html5rocks.com/*)

HTML5 Safari Technology Overview by Apple (*http://developer.apple.com/technolo gies/safari/html5.html*)

Periodic Table of HTML5 Elements (*http://joshduck.com/periodic-table.html*)

HTML5 Demos and Examples (*http://html5demos.com/*)

HTML5 Tracker (*http://html5.org/tools/web-apps-tracker*)

HTML5 Visual Cheat Sheet (*http://woork.blogspot.com/2009/09/html-5-visual-cheat -sheet-by-woork.html*)

SwitchToHTML5 - The HTML5 Framework Generator (*http://switchtohtml5.com/*)

Creating Cross Browser HTML5 Forms Now, Using modernizr, webforms2 and html5Widgets (*http://www.useragentman.com/blog/2010/07/27/cross-browser -html5-forms-using-modernizr-webforms2-and-html5widgets/*)

HTML5 Test (*http://html5test.com/*)

HTML5 Canvas Cheat Sheet (*http://blog.nihilogic.dk/2009/02/html5-canvas-cheat -sheet.html*)

Interactive Experiments focused on HTML5 (*http://hakim.se/experiments*)

HTML5 Please - Use the new and shiny responsibly (*http://html5please.com/*)

Websites about CSS3

CSS3 Please! Cross-Browser CSS3 Rule Generator (*http://css3please.com/*)

LESS << The Dynamic Stylesheet Language (*http://lesscss.org/*)

Sass - Syntactically Awesome Stylesheets (*http://sass-lang.com/*)

ZUSS (ZK User-interface Style Sheet) (*https://github.com/tomyeh/ZUSS*)

XCSS - OO CSS Framework (*http://xcss.antpaw.org/*)

Websites about JavaScript

JavaScript only three "bad" parts (*http://johnkpaul.tumblr.com/post/20720951024/java script-only-three-bad-parts*)

Web Inspector: Understanding Stack Traces (*http://www.webkit.org/blog/1544/web-in spector-understanding-stack-traces/*)

Understanding JavaScript OOP (*http://killdream.github.com/blog/2011/10/understand ing-javascript-oop/*)

Understanding JavaScript's this Keyword (*http://javascriptweblog.wordpress.com/ 2010/08/30/understanding-javascripts-this/*)

Other Frameworks

Cappuccino (*http://cappuccino.org/*)

SproutCore (*http://www.sproutcore.com/*)

jQTouch (*http://jqtouch.com/*)

zepto.js (*http://zeptojs.com/*)

iUI (*http://code.google.com/p/iui/*)

Initializr (*http://www.initializr.com/*)

HTML5 Reset (*http://html5reset.org/*)

iWebKit (*http://snippetspace.com/*)

LimeJS (*http://www.limejs.com/*)

WebApp.net (*http://webapp-net.com/*)

Jo (*http://joapp.com/*)

About the Author

Adrian Kosmaczewski has been working as an iOS developer since 2008. Before that, he was a web developer working with classic ASP since 1996, ASP.NET, PHP, Ruby on Rails, Django, and more. He runs a consulting and training business in Oron-la-Ville, Switzerland. He has a degree of Master of Science in Information Technology from the University of Liverpool.

Have it your way.

Get even more for your money.

Join the O'Reilly Community, and register the O'Reilly books you own. It's free, and you'll get:

- $4.99 ebook upgrade offer
- 40% upgrade offer on O'Reilly print books
- Membership discounts on books and events
- Free lifetime updates to ebooks and videos
- Multiple ebook formats, DRM FREE
- Participation in the O'Reilly community
- Newsletters
- Account management
- 100% Satisfaction Guarantee

Signing up is easy:

1. Go to: oreilly.com/go/register
2. Create an O'Reilly login.
3. Provide your address.
4. Register your books.

Note: English-language books only

To order books online:
oreilly.com/store

For questions about products or an order:
orders@oreilly.com

To sign up to get topic-specific email announcements and/or news about upcoming books, conferences, special offers, and new technologies:
elists@oreilly.com

For technical questions about book content:
booktech@oreilly.com

To submit new book proposals to our editors:
proposals@oreilly.com

O'Reilly books are available in multiple DRM-free ebook formats. For more information:
oreilly.com/ebooks

O'REILLY®

Spreading the knowledge of innovators

oreilly.com

Lightning Source UK Ltd.
Milton Keynes UK
UKHW031508111021
392023UK00006B/280